Scots Wha Hae!

BREAKING NEWS FROM SCOTLAND'S PAST

Alasdair Anderson
Douglas McNaughton
Martin Coventry

GOBLINSHEAD
Musselburgh

Scots Wha Hae!

First Published 2001
© Alasdair Anderson, Douglas McNaughton
and Martin Coventry 2001

Published by GOBLINSHEAD
130B Inveresk Road
Musselburgh EH21 7AY Scotland
tel 0131 665 2894; *fax* 0131 653 6566
email goblinshead@sol.co.uk

British Library Cataloguing in Publication Data
A catalogue record for this book is available from the
British Library.

ISBN 1 899874 35 6

Typeset by GOBLINSHEAD using Desktop Publishing

*If you would like a colour catalogue of our
publications please contact the publishers at*
**Goblinshead, 130B Inveresk Road,
Musselburgh EH21 7AY, Scotland, UK.**

COMING SOON ...

Jurassic Glen
Could Dinosaurs Still Roam the Highlands?
by Diana J Weinstein III

**The Scottish Guide to the Strange and Funny World of
Unexplained Things**
by Diana J Weinstein III

Scottish Culture: A Contradiction in Terms?
by Dr Ceilidh Minogue

Introduction

This book began life as 'a tabloid view of Scottish history' but in the writing process it developed into something more. It evolved into a series of articles culled from the pages of imaginary papers such as *The Daily Chippie* and *The Sunday Scone*. A modern-day perspective on events is occasionally offered by the crazed academic Dr Ceilidh Minogue, angry letters from the Brunt family, or the postcards of credulous tourist Diana J Weinstein III.

Not all of the news stories could be rewritten to be amusing, so in the pages that follow you may have trouble separating history from humour. We certainly wouldn't recommend anyone to use this book as a revision aid for exams! However, there is a lot of factual research included in the book, so you might learn things you didn't know about Scotland, and have a good laugh in the process. We did.

AA, DMcN, MC
May 2001

Acknowledgements
"City Plague Street Sealed" on page 65 is based on an original pizza with Adam S Woods. Thanks also to Joyce Miller and Peter and Jackie for unearthing fragments of Burns poems and taking them to the Globe Inn in Dumfries.

Scottish History 'more interesting' - and that's official!

SCOTTISH HISTORY is officially more interesting than anyone else's - because it's been destroyed.

That's the claim of Scottish historians, who announced their findings after a week-long conference at Skibo Castle.

Scottish history was stolen by Edward I, who made off with all Scotland's official records and, after the Treaty of Boroughmuir, gave them all back again. However when the Scots saw 300 years of filing sailing into port, plucky nationalists swam out with small axes, holed the boat, and the paperwork of Scottish history slipped into the bay. The wholesale destruction of Scottish history has had a remarkably exciting side-effect.

It means that, unlike English historians, who kept every last receipt and rendered their history embarrassingly factual, Scottish historians have the option to

- **DISAGREE** incessantly over everything
- **SPECULATE** airily til the cows come home
- **ARGUE THE TOSS** over every single point, no matter how minor
- **DISPUTE** the accepted view of every historical event, even really important ones

A Scottish historian said yesterday 'English history is carefully preserved and the whole thing is like a great epic story told in minute detail and it is the dullest thing on God's earth. Scottish history is so controversial. You can build an entire career out of meaningless speculation about the smallest points. And in historical debates, if you have no concrete evidence, you can just make stuff up. It's great. I love being a Scottish historian, me.'

Job centres have reported a rush of people applying to become Scottish historians since this announcement was made in a pub.

Scots Wha Hae!

Famous Scottish Songs
As sung by most Scots

Scots Wha Hae

Scots wha hae wi' Wallace bled
Scots wham Bruce has often led
De de de de de de de
De de de de de!
De de de de de de de
De de de de de de de
De de de de de de de
De de de de de!

De de de de de de de
De de de de de de de
De de de de de de de
De de de de de!
De de de de de de de
De de de de de de de
De de de de de de de
De de de de de!

De de de de de de de
De de de de de de de
De de de de de de de
De de de de de!
De de de de de de de
De de de de de de de
De de de de de de de
De de de de de!

ADVERTISEMENT

Looking for somewhere to settle?
Come to

Scotland

If you thought Scotland was a frozen wasteland, think again! The recent melting of the glaciers over Scotland has revealed a rugged and striking new land mass ready to move into. The melt water has created lochs and the climate has encouraged rapid growth of forests - already fully stocked with livestock. If you like red deer, wild boar and ox, this is the country for you!

Have Your Own Living Space

Whatever your taste in accommodation, Scotland offers the residence of your choice. There are ample penthouse caves with commanding views over the dramatic unspoilt landscape. Or there is ample space for development - you can design and create your own luxury prefab apartments of sticks and animal hides. Or perhaps you are seeking a top-of-the-range hut built with the very latest stone-breaking techniques. No problem! There's stone all over the place.

Eating Out

As well as the forest livestock and the amply stocked rivers and lakes, Scotland is completely vegetarian friendly! Roots, wild grains and berries are widely available - so there's always a choice.

The Good Life

Whether you are a conventional hunter-gatherer, or at the cutting edge of settlement creation, Scotland is rich in opportunities. There are packs of wild dogs just ready to tame to help you in your hunting. The total lack of any previous farming means the virgin ground is ready to burst forth with crops. State-of-the-art flint axes supplied to first 100 settlers.

Make it - in Scotland

THE STONE AGE SCOTLAND DEVELOPMENT BOARD © 8000 BC
www.stoneagescotland.co.uk

Need an axe? Come to Creag-Na-Caillich ...

Quality Axes from Perthshire

A range of uses
* Clear the land *
* Cut trees for construction *
* Kill wild animals *
* Dispose of quarrelsome neighbours *

Visit our trading site in the Northeast or buy direct from the factory in Perthshire
(10% factory discount)

The Creag-Na-Caillich Seal of Quality
Finest Perthshire Stone
Remember - we don't make axes for anyone else

Trading terms
In exchange for our axes we accept pottery, hides, seed, food and Caledonian Express

Coming soon: 'Knives'! Want to find out more?
Join our mailing list.
Send your address to: Creag-Na-Caillich, Perthshire

Council Row Over Skara Brae Plans

ORKNEY COUNCIL is embroiled in a row over Skara Brae development plans put on display this week. The plans, on view at the Council office (by the cave mouth), show a major development of up to ten houses.

Local residents say the development:

* **Will spoil the Bay of Skail's natural beauty**
* **Could damage the tourist industry from Scandinavia**
* **Has been planned with insufficient consultation**
* **Uses unproven technology**

Mr Og, an architect for the scheme, claimed today 'How can the development spoil the view? It's all going to be underground. And we're using natural materials like stone and whalebone to be environmentally friendly. It's a cutting-edge development and these moaning minnies are living in the Stone Age.' When we pointed out that that was exactly what they were doing, he became tight-lipped and said 'no further comment'.

Costs for the scheme are already thought to be spiralling out of control; plans show that the lavishly appointed apartments will have fires, drains and even furniture. Architects have claimed that the drainage and sanitation arrangements are state of the art and will not be emulated for thousands of years.

Concerns that foreigners could move into the area – some of them from as far away as five miles – have already been aired.

Jim Og, a prominent local resident, said: 'I've lived here all my life and have never needed to go further than a mile from where I was born. Next thing you know we'll have all these incomers settling here.

'There goes the neighbourhood.'

The plans themselves were also roundly denounced, with the radical new building techniques coming in for criticism: 'Whalebone and stone? I ask you. They won't last five minutes, never mind 5000 years,' said local spaewife, Granny Og.

Councillor Og, in charge of the scheme, was today unavailable to speak to us.

Ideal Tomb Exhibition

ORKNEY WAS in the news again today after the grand opening of Maes Howe, the architectural wonder of the age. This impressive mausoleum has just been completed by local craftsmen, and Orkney dignitaries joined with press to admire the achievement. An appreciative crowd nibbled on canapés of lobster, oysters, mussel and crab – traditional local fare - before the tour of Maes Howe itself.

The exterior of the cairn towers above surrounding dwellings, with a massive facade dominated by its entrance stone. As we entered the narrow entrance passage we were impressed by the long, smooth slabs which form the walls. The passage is cunningly aligned to the south-west, lined up with the midwinter sunset. On the shortest day of the year, the rays of the sun shine directly in and illuminate the back wall of the burial chamber.

The spacious inner chamber is roughly square with each corner formed by a massive standing stone. The walls come together above to create a soaring stone ceiling. Three small side cells can be seen in the walls, designed as resting places for the dead.

This magnificent monument took 40,000 man-hours to complete. The feat of quarrying and transporting the stone was in itself impressive.

Maes Howe will stand as enduring testament to our respect for our honoured dead.

The word in architectural circles is that the Egyptians are thinking of something similar; but how can their 'pyramids' rival Maes Howe?

Comment

Go On Home, Johnny Pict!

For too long, we have turned a blind eye to the hooliganism of Pictish visitors. For the sake of the tourist industry we have put up with their loutish ways.

They SWAGGER about in their tribes, RAID our settlements, RAPE and PILLAGE our communities.

They have taken our lands and nothing was said. Just a polite memo to their embassy. All for another piece of iron for the tourist board.

Well this political correctness has gone too far!

Their aggressive and reckless behaviour shows that there's only one language these Pictish pillocks understand.

Brute force.

So you can stick your enigmatic carved monoliths where the sun don't shine.

MEMO

To: Agricola, in charge of the Roman legions in the new
territory of north Britain across the German Sea

From: The Emperor Domitian

Subject: The Caledonian hordes

Dear Agricola

After seven years in the new territory I am disappointed that you have not
had much success in subduing the natives. You told me that they were
divided, always fighting amongst themselves and having tribal wars and
sectarian disputes. Well they seem to be better organised than you made out.
I have information to the effect that chieftains who were formerly at each
others' throats are banding together and they have raised an army of thirty
thousand men. They've formed a unified state which has been blessed by
their priests and are ready to risk everything to liberate their country. I am
not best pleased that our forces have never been north of the Forth, that your
front line has been stationary for five years, and that your best efforts consist
of border skirmishes. A few burnt-out villages do not, to my mind, constitute
a glorious campaign. I've heard enough excuses about how terrible the
weather is and how you have to retrench during the winter months. I don't
need to tell you that if we get kicked out by a bunch of hairy-legged
heathens it will be a PR disaster, so it is time to launch a major offensive.
Get the finger out and sort out those ginger nuts - pronto.

MEMO

To: The Emperor Domitian

From: Agricola

cc: Tacitus, Roman Empire PR Department

Subject: The Battle of Mons Graupius

Thank you for your note. In an attempt to subjugate
the Caledonians once and for all, I formed the army
into three divisions, and began the march to the
north. We crossed the territory between the Forth and
the Tay without incident. At the same time I commanded
the fleet to cruise on the coast, and strike terror by
devastating the parts within its reach.

When we reached the valley of the Tay the soldiers
exclaimed 'Ecce Tiberim!' Felt quite at home - it
looks just like the valley of the Tiber. Beyond the
Tay, and stretching almost clear across the country,
is the 'Great Strath', a plain with the Sidlaws in the
south and the Grampians in the north. Towards the
north of the plain, we encountered the native forces
at a place I'll call 'Mons Graupius' (see enclosed
map).

MEMO

To: Agricola
From: The Emperor Domitian

Your map got lost (I mopped up my wine with it). Can you do another one?
We don't want people forever wondering where this encounter took place.

MEMO

To: The Emperor Domitian
From: Agricola

Can I just make a point? Italy is great. The
weather is really good, there's tons of food, and
everybody has a tan. This new country is rubbish.
The weather is terrible, everyone is starving, and
the inhabitants are a bunch of barbarian savages.

What the hell are we doing here????

Hand-written annotation: Torn up and never sent.

MEMO

To: The Emperor Domitian
From: Agricola
cc: Roman Empire PR Department, Tacitus

As we approached the native force, we could see
they were armed with the simplest of weapons and
boy were their knees knocking. You could tell they
had never seen the like. Our legions were magnificent beneath their ensigns and eagles, in the
splendour of their mail, brazen shields gleaming,
the very might of the Empire itself embodied in her
finest sons etc. etc. (Tacitus - lard it on here.)

(Note: with 26,000 to their 30,000 we were ever
so slightly outnumbered. But I did lose count about
the 27,500 mark so I might be a bit out with my
figures.)

In the open space between the armies the Caledonians start to show off their war chariots. You
wouldn't believe these things. It's the crudest
contraption of a wooden seat and two metal wheels.
They have scythes projecting from the axles and
it's pulled by a horse with the combatant in the
seat. Real 'boy racer' stuff.

Anyway at the head of the assembled Caledonian
tribes was their appointed leader, Calgacus. The
histories should show that Calgacus delivered a

rousing speech. Tacitus - make something good up
here.   Something along the lines of 'There is now
no nation beyond us, nothing save the billows and
the rocks, and the Romans, still more savage, whose
tyranny you will in vain appease by submission and
concession. The devastators of the earth, when the
land has failed to suffice their universal ravages,
they explore even the ocean. If an enemy be
wealthy, they are covetous; if he be poor, they
become ambitious. Neither East nor West has con-
tented them. Alone, of all men, they covet with
equal rapacity the rich and the needy. Plunder,
murder, and robbery, under false pretences they
call 'empire', and when they make a wilderness,
they call it 'peace'.'

   In point of actual fact all we heard was something that sounded like 'You're going home in an
ambulance', but that's a bit less noble.

   Now it is my turn to address my troops, rousing
them to the heights of loyalty to the glorious
Roman Empire! (Full transcript follows with next
report).

MEMO

To: Agricola
From: The Emperor Domitian

I don't pay you to stand around all day making speeches. Get fighting or
you're sacked!

MEMO

To: The Emperor Domitian
From: Agricola
cc: Roman Empire PR Department, Tacitus

I assembled my troops into two lines, with auxil-
iary infantry in the first, three thousand horse in
the wings, and the Roman legionaries in the second
line (as per recent memo about using the foreigners
as sword fodder and keeping the Romans to the back
to preserve the flower of our army).

   The battle began at a distance, with the Caledo-

nians firing showers of flint arrowheads. With our
army giving way, I ordered three cohorts of Batavians and two of Tungrians to close with the foe and
bring the encounter to the sword. The Caledonians
met them, shouting their war-cry, but the change in
the battle placed them at great disadvantage. Their
long swords were unsuitable for close combat and
their little round shields (I'll bring one back as
a souvenir, for a laugh) were next to useless. Fair
play to them, they met us head-on with a great war-
cry (the ambulance thing again) but the tide was
turning. Our troops were superbly equipped for
hand-to-hand encounter with the standard issue
short sword and long shield. The barbarian apes
should be despatched within hours and Caledonia
will be ours. I'll keep you posted.

MEMO

To: The Emperor Domitian
From: Agricola
Subject: A bit later

It's all happening here. The Batavians totally lost
the place (as usual) dashing the knobs of their
bucklers in the faces of the Caledonians, and
stabbing them with their short swords, forcing them
back towards the hills. However, they got a bit
carried away in their eagerness to press forward
and left behind them many natives who had not
actually been injured. They all got up and started
fighting again, now within our own lines. To add to
the chaos, the chariots became entangled with the
fighting infantry. You can imagine it - the horses
panic and career wildly over the field, the scythes
on the chariot wheels mowing down any in their
path. What a shambles!

The next thing is, the reserves in the hills rush
down with seeming intent to outflank us. I had been
too clever for them though. Four battalions of
cavalry, kept in reserve till this moment, met and
subdued their advance. And at this point I ordered
the wings of our forces to push forward and enclose
the Caledonian army. The natives were at our mercy.
The day was ours and the plain ran red with Caledonian blood.

MEMO

```
To:       The Emperor Domitian
From:     Agricola
P.S.   This is an interesting bit - remember I had
ordered the fleet in the German Sea to keep pace
with the troops? After the battle the ships held on
their way to the north, and entering the Pentland
Firth, sailed westward into the Atlantic. They
sailed round the northern point, and confirmed for
certain our assumption that Britain is an island.
In this expedition we discovered a cluster of
islands called the Orcades - another addition to
the Roman empire.
```

MEMO

To: Agricola

From: The Emperor Domitian

Well that's more like it. At last, results. Now make sure you kill all the survivors. The last thing we need is any hint of nationalist feeling lingering. It will cause nothing but trouble.

MEMO

To: Roman Empire Marketing Department

From: The Emperor Domitian

While Agricola is faffing about securing our new territory, we have to give it a name. I have looked through the list of suggestions you gave me and frankly I was not impressed. Here are my views.

Pictavia: apparently, some of them are known as 'Picts' because they paint themselves with pictures. You'll have to do better than that.

Caledonia: Now the Caledonii are that warlike lot in Perthshire. I am having a lot of trouble with them. Therefore this name seems too nationalistic.

Alba: Apparently this is the Gaelic name for the region occupied by the Scotti – another lot of trouble makers. I'm not having it named after a Gaelic word because that will just make the Gaelic language a rallying call for the nationalistic malcontents and they'll want their own telly programmes in it. Hardly anyone speaks it anyway.

Votadiniland: the Votadini are a crappo tribe in Lothian and their heads are big enough. We are not naming it after them. They'll start thinking they should get the capital city next.

Get your thinking caps on - while you still have heads to wear them on!

HAND-WRITTEN ANNOTATION:

Sod it, let's just call the whole thing 'Britain' and have done with it

```
So began 2000 years of cultural identity crisis...
```

Comment

Go On Home, Johnny Roman!

For too long, we have turned a blind eye to the hooliganism of Italian visitors. For the sake of the tourist industry we have put up with their loutish ways.

They SWAGGER about in their phalanxes, RAID our hill forts, RAPE and PILLAGE our communities.

They slaughtered our peace-loving ambassadors at Mons Graupius and nothing was said. Just a polite memo to the Roman embassy. All for another piece of Lira for the tourist board.

<u>Well this political correctness has gone too far!</u>

The bloodbath at Mons Graupius shows that there's only one language these Latin lunatics understand.

Brute force.

<u>So you can stick your centurions where the sun don't shine.</u>

Walls to you, Hadrian!

It may be big, but it's not clever. Take your wall and take a hike.

Scots say no to wall!

It's an eyesore and should be moved. Why don't they put their wall up next to London? We interviewed residents around Chesters and they were unanimous in their opposition to the wall.

'The price of hovels has gone right down since they put that bloody thing there,' said Tom Son of Tom, root gatherer, 22. 'I mean who wants to live next to a thing like that. It's spoilt the view and you can't get a wink of sleep with those Roman soldiers rattling their armour all night and marching about in formation. Who do they think they are: the bloody Londinium ballet?'

Key Fact

Pontius Pilate is said to have been born at Fortingall, near Aberfeldy in Perthshire, son of a Roman soldier and a Caledonian woman.

Disappointing Successor to Hadrian's Wall Opens
Antonine Wall Draws Small Crowd

Tam, Son of Tom, was among the meagre crowd. His father had lived next to the original wall so he was keen to see the new landmark, the so-called Antonine Wall, today.

'It's a bit dull and not a patch on the original. My father used to complain all the time about the wall that Hadrian built. But that was a proper defensive fortification, I don't think he'd bother wasting his breath about this one.'

'My granddad could overrun it,' added his wife Senga, 'and he's 52!'

So it's the thumbs down all round for Antonius Pius's new construction. This wall won't be winning him many points in the toughest world emperor competition.

Lost and Found
Missing: Legion. Goes by the title of Ninth. Likes marching and hot baths. If found please return to Roman Emperor.

Comment

Go On Home, Johnny Scot!

For too long, we have turned a blind eye to the hooliganism of Irish visitors.

For the sake of the tourist industry we have put up with their loutish ways.

They SWAGGER about in their coracles, RAID our hill forts, RAPE and PILLAGE our communities.

They stole and settled our lands in the west and nothing was said. Just a polite memo to the Irish embassy. All for another piece of Punt for the tourist board.

Well this political correctness has gone too far!

Their Christian ways show that there's only one language these Irish imbeciles understand.

<u>Brute force.</u>

So you can stick your Stone of Destiny where the sun don't shine.

Columba in Water Beast Probe

CONTROVERSY SURROUNDED Saint Columba yesterday after it was claimed that he had encountered a water beast in Loch Ness.

It is believed that the saint was travelling to visit the Pictish king when his party paused by the shores of the Loch. Seeing a large water beast bearing down on a swimmer in the loch, Columba raised his hand and invoked the name of God. Eyewitnesses report that he commanded the monster to 'go back with all speed'. The beast complied, and the swimmer was saved.

The high-profile Columba is no stranger to controversy. He became the darling of the paparazzi after he was instrumental in introducing Christianity to Scotland. And he was embroiled in a copyright battle after unlawfully copying a set of the Gospels in his homeland of Ireland. But this latest scandal looks set to be a monster one.

LONELY HEARTS

Nessie

A trim four tons, this well-preserved 65-million-year-old lady seeks male plesiosaur for friendship, maybe more. Likes: swimming and fish. Dislikes: being photographed.

Postcards from the Old Country by Diana J. Weinstein III

Yesterday I visited Loch Ness. Really wanted to see the monster but after a couple of hours it was getting cold. Fortunately the landlady in my guest house had provided a 'wee dram' of brandy so had some of that to keep warm. No sign of the monster. Went for lunch and the waitress suggested I have some 'tartan special'. Well it didn't taste very special to me. When I went back to watch the Loch (that's Gaelic for 'loch' and means a landlocked lake) some fishermen gave me some of their whisky. And then, would you believe it, as I was looking at the water I saw blurry, indistinct shapes! Could it have been Nessie?

Diana

Tourist Lay-by and Recycling Bin, Drumnadrochit

Druid Slams New Age Cult

DRUIDS HAVE WARNED parents against what they allege is a dangerous new cult to emerge from the Continent.

'These people must be stopped,' said the Head Druid Briochan (45) from his sacred grove near Urquhart on Loch Ness. 'These people are dangerous and our children must be protected. Not only is our traditional way of life being threatened but they are introducing practices which can harm people and wildlife alike, and turn children against parents.'

Briochan has cited a series of bizarre events which have been attributed to this new cult, the Christians, with their zealous missionaries and saints.

These include:

- **St Serf slew a perfectly serviceable dragon in the Dragon Hole at Kinnoull**

- **St Moluag cut off his little finger and threw it on to the island of Lismore: then claiming Lismore for his own**

- **St Barr converted the folk of Barra and persuaded them to stop cannibalism**

- **St Mungo of Glasgow brought a dead robin back to life, used a stag and wolf to plough a field, and sowed a field with sand but grew a fine crop of wheat**

- **St Columba terrified a friendly kelpie or water horse, our very own Nessie, in Loch Ness**

- **St Triduana plucked out her own eyes and sent them to an admirer on a skewer**

Briochan went on: 'Not only are these Christians abusing our local wildlife, endangering rare species such as dragons and kelpies, but it is our young people I really worry about.

'St Triduana claims to be a virgin, and has now mutilated herself. What kind of example is this? What is she saying? That it is OK to pluck out your own eyes rather than being courted by a man? That being a virgin is desirable?'

Meanwhile the prominent Christian St Columba, from his monastery on Iona, hit back: 'The druids are very complacent, and conveniently forget their own history of human sacrifice, excess and indulgence. While it is true that some of our supporters have possibly taken things a bit far, it is because of their enthusiasm for the Truth and the Word.

'After all, we offer eternal life in a wonderful paradise, free from disease, hunger, pestilence and death. In this Dark Age of barbarism and continual strife, what have the druids got that can match that?'

Comment

Go On Home, Johnny Angle!

For too long, we have turned a blind eye to the hooliganism of German visitors.

For the sake of the tourist industry we have put up with their loutish ways.

They SWAGGER about in their hordes, RAID our fortresses, RAPE and PILLAGE our communities.

They stole and settled our lands in the south and nothing was said. Just a polite memo to the German embassy. All for another piece of Merk for the tourist board.

<u>Well this political correctness has gone too far!</u>

Their heathen ways show that there's only one language these German jokers understand.

Brute force.

<u>So you can stick your bratwurst where the sun don't shine.</u>

Victory at Nechtansmere

THE PICTS scored a major victory over the Angles this week at the battle of Nechtansmere.

For some years, the Angles of Northumberland have been pushing northwards and putting pressure on their neighbours, the Britons of Strathclyde, the Scots of Dalriada, and the Picts to the north of the river Forth.

In 638 they captured Dun Eidyn, known as Edinburgh to some, and over the following decades have exerted more and more control over the southern Picts.

In recent years, King Brudei of the Picts has been sending guerrilla-style raiding parties into Northumbria.

King Ecgfrith of Northumbria invaded Pictland in retaliation, only to be drawn into a trap by a pretended Pictish withdrawal. Lured into the area between the hill fort of Dun Nechtan and a swamp known as Nechtans Mire (or Mere), the Northumbrian force was defeated.

Reports are garbled, but what is clear is that King Ecgfrith and his bodyguard have been killed, and the Northumbrian army was routed, most of them slain or enslaved.

Thus the 'English influence' retreated south of the River Forth, and the Battle of Nechtansmere was a triumph for the Picts.

It is a resounding victory for King Brudei, but what does it mean for Pictland? It is a victory not just in military terms, but also in political terms, preserving the integrity of Pictish culture and society.

The Picts have breathing room to extend their influence south again, and dominate Dalriada.

Major carved stones have been commissioned at Aberlemno to commemorate the battle.

King Brudei is reported to be disappointed by the stones. He told this paper: 'This is one of the most important events in our history, nay, within the whole history of Scotland. If we had lost, the kingdom of Scots would probably never have emerged. And all we'll get are some enigmatic carved stones that nobody understands and a mention in the chronicles of the time. Jings and crivvens.

'What about a fine tapestry depicting the events?'

Iona Sacked
by Vikings
No Survivors in Pillage of Western Isles

VIKINGS have sacked the monastery at Iona and devastated the entire community, it was revealed today.

The Iona community has been a beacon of sanctity ever since Christianity was brought to these shores. However, the recent attack has left the community devastated and it is feared that there are no survivors.

In their distinctive eagle-headed ships, Vikings have been a familiar sight round our shores since 787. It is thought that they are attracted to religious institutions in search of riches held by these bodies. In 793 they overran the church at Lindisfarne, laying it waste, digging up the altars, and carrying off all the treasures of the holy church. Eyewitnesses claim that the Viking marauders killed some of the brethren, drowned some in the sea, and carried others off in chains.

Iona had for five generations been a model community and a centre of learning and culture unparalleled in the modern world. The school there has long been a favourite for the sons of princes and nobles. Scholars from abroad flocked to its shore. And kings, when dying, commanded that their bones should be transported across the North Sea, and laid to rest on the island of Iona.

The attack on Iona has left none of the inhabitants alive. After loading their ships with the spoils of the attack, the Vikings destroyed all that they were unable to carry away and departed, leaving the western isles a scene of desolation.

Key Fact

Scotland's famed history of heart disease is probably the fault of the Vikings. They had cholesterol-rich diets in order to cope with extreme cold and sudden demands for energy. Around 1200 years ago Viking settlers began to intermarry with Scots, introducing this factor into the gene pool, particularly in the north.

COMMENT

Go On Home, Johnny Viking!

For too long, we have turned a blind eye to the hooliganism of Scandinavian visitors. For the sake of the tourist industry we have put up with their loutish ways.

<u>They SWAGGER about in their longships, RAID our monasteries, RAPE and PILLAGE our communities.</u>

They devastated the monastery at Iona and nothing was said. Just a polite memo to the Danish embassy. All for another piece of Kroner for the tourist board.

Well this political correctness has gone too far!

The sacking of the community at Iona shows that there's only one language these Nordic nitwits understand.

Brute force.

<u>So you can stick your horned helmets where the sun don't shine.</u>

21

King Kenny!

Kenneth MacAlpin Unites Scots and Picts

'WHAT A LOAD of rubbish you read in the papers these days. I was glancing over one the other day and it claimed that I'd slaughtered all the Picts at a special supper. Stuff and nonsense! I'm very good friends with the Picts; in fact they even invited me to be their king. We get on very well, oh yes indeed, and we are building up a special relationship within a unified Scotland. Yes, me and the Picts are good mates and often go out for a drink.'

I spoke to King Kenneth MacAlpin the other day at his capital of Forteviot. He came across as a man with a vision.

'I'd like to be seen as the man who united Scotland under the one banner. Pict and Scot living together like brothers. These are harsh times and life is cheap. Maybe there were a few accidental injuries but the creation of the Scottish nation was worth a few bruises and grazes.'

Meanwhile, Angus, last of the Pictish royal house has refuted this claim, saying: 'You lying swine, Kenneth MacAlpin, you did murder them and just after the appetisers. I only escaped because I had a bad bout of Ecgfrith's Revenge. It's just not fair! We were once a proud and war-like people.

'And we did carve some rather fine, albeit enigmatic, stones.'

23

Macbeth Felled in Birnam Wood

Malcolm Canmore Victorious at Dunsinane: English Support Canmore

TRAGIC news for Scotland. Our good king, Macbeth, has been treacherously defeated by Malcolm Canmore, son of the discredited Duncan, with English help.

Macbeth and his allies were resting peacefully at his palace at Dunsinane. Malcolm and his English supporters disguised themselves as Birnam Wood, wantonly cutting down the trees of that ancient forest. They sneaked up on the palace and surprised the thrice-ennobled Macbeth.

Macbeth had no option to leg it, and has been toppled by Malcolm Canmore. Canmore is now king in the south, although glorious Macbeth still rules in Moray and the north.

An environmental spokesman for Birnam Wood said: 'The damage is terrible. One day, little of Scotland's native forests will remain. This is destruction on a ferocious scale: trees chopped down, branches hacked off, saplings severely depressed. Macbeth maybe had his faults, but nobody has accused him of needless destruction of trees, deforestation and global warming.'

Macbeth Wins Libel Case

The final verdict from the big libel trial Macbeth vs. Shakespeare was announced today. Macbeth has proved his case. Shakespeare had portrayed him as a hen-pecked man who was talked into murdering his king, to whom he owed allegiance, by his domineering wife.

'That bloody play of his: it's all a pack of lies, he just made it all up and I proved it in court. For a start I've been ruling for 16 years. Which as most Scottish monarchs seem to only survive a couple of months, proves I must be a pretty good king. All this rubbish about me killing the ancient Duncan. Yes I

Macbeth Wins Libel Case
continued from page 26

continued from page 26

admit I did kill him! OK, OK I'll take the rap for that although it was in battle and he had attacked me first in his usual cowardly way. But he wasn't old, he was a lot younger than me and had it coming to him because he was a snotty little oik. Nor did I murder Banquo, as he never even existed except in the imagination of some brown-nosing chronicler trying to suck up to later kings; and MacDuff, his wife and babes were dear friends and even came to our wedding.'

'To be quite honest I had as much right to be king as he did. That's the way we do it in Scotland. There's this thing called Tanistry. It means that there's always an adult king on the throne. The succession goes down the line through male relations, not just sons. I have to admit it is a bit of a bugger since there is always someone wanting a go on the throne while the current king is still alive.'

'But just because I killed a relative, there was no reason for this inept hack to put together a farrago of lies and half-truths that have blackened my name no end. And the witches? Witches, I ask you? In this day and age! My God, I even went on pilgrimage to Rome and distributed monies among the poor.'

'I'd like to thank my wife for standing beside me in this difficult time.'

We managed to have a word with the losing defendant Mr W. Shakespeare of Stratford: 'So, Will? Disappointed?'

'I'm as queasy as a partridge at the result. We thought we had a great case. But you've got to get on with your life. You win some, you lose some. Hopefully we can put this behind us. As it is I've got a new play coming out about these two sets of twins, it's a laugh-a-minute farce, full of mistaken identities and hilarious misunderstanding. And there might even be some nudity. So book your ticket now.'

Some commentators have suggested that this libel case was just a cynical publicity exercise to sell more seats. This paper wouldn't like to comment on that.

Macbeth said: 'This has taught that Shakespeare a lesson. This play should be consigned to the waste bin of history. Now whose version will be remembered?'

COMMENT

Go On Home, Johnny Norman!

For too long, we have turned a blind eye to the hooliganism of French visitors. For the sake of the tourist industry we have put up with their loutish ways.

They SWAGGER about in their chain mail, RAID our strongholds, RAPE and PILLAGE our communities.

They raided the south of Scotland under William the Conqueror and nothing was said. Just a polite memo to the French embassy. All for another piece of Franc for the tourist board.

<u>Well this political correctness has gone too far!</u>

Their raiding ways show that there's only one language these French fancies understand.

<u>Brute force.</u>

So you can stick your motte and bailey where the sun don't shine.

Canmore Slain at Alnwick

Spear from Birnam Wood Blamed

MALCOLM III has been murdered at Alnwick in Northumberland. Our king believed he was receiving the surrender of the castle and town. The keys were offered to him on the end of a spear. As he went to take them, Malcolm Canmore was run through and slain. His eldest son and heir, Edward, has also died from his wounds at Alnwick.

In a bizarre twist of events the spear used to kill Malcolm has been shown to come from Birnam Wood. 'I enjoyed my revenge,' said the spear. 'Malcolm was responsible for the killing of many trees in Birnam, including my family. I survived, and grew strong and straight. It took many years to track down the murderers of my people, but now I feel at peace.'

'That's one in the eye for all those who would desecrate nature,' added the spear. 'Incidentally, one of my relatives got Harold at Hastings.'

Lay Off Queen Margaret!

The death of Malcolm has led to mean-spirited attacks on Queen Margaret. There are those who say she made Scotland too English. And that her influence reformed the Celtic church.

<u>We say - and about time too!</u>

Scotland has to move forward. If feudalism is the way ahead, so be it.

And the Celtic Church? It needed reform. Its customs were archaic and needed to be brought into line with the Church of Rome. And its structures and practices were highly irregular.

The Queen has been good for the church. She encouraged the veneration of native saints. She ordered the restoration of the monastery at Iona, which had fallen into disrepair. And she gave liberally to the clerical communities known as the Culdees, who strive for greater strictness in the Celtic Church.

We should see her as saint, not sinner.

Let's Put the Scot Back Into Scotland

THE DEATH of Malcolm III, known to us all as Canmore, has led to scenes of mourning throughout the land.

But let's not get carried away. The king was more English than the English at times. He brought their customs into the country at the expense of our own ways. In fact he needed English help to defeat our last dear king Macbeth.

He paid homage to his Celtic forebears. But he spoke more English and French than Gaelic.

And look who he married. First Ingibjorg - a Norse princess all the way from Orkney! Then Margaret - sister of the last contender to the English throne from the Anglo-Saxon house of Wessex, raised in Hungary, and later a visitor to the French-loving court of Edward the Confessor. She's been around.

Look at the names she gave her sons. Anglo-Saxon names: Edward, Edgar, Edmund, Ethelred, Alexander and David. Not a MacAlpin name among them. No wonder they're known as the Margaretsons.

We say - get rid of these mummy's boys!

Malcolm's brother Donald Ban has the right idea. He has banished Malcolm's sons from his kingdom. If they think England's so great they can stay there.

Donald has succeeded to the throne thanks to the time-honoured Celtic inheritance rules which favour brothers over sons. Just as the MacAlpin kings did, he has divided his power, allowing one of Malcolm's sons, Edmund, to remain here and rule Lothian and Strathclyde on his behalf. Donald will rule over Scotia, north of the Forth, the very heart of our nation.

'Scotland Fairly Peaceful' Shock

SCOTLAND has been fairly peaceful for the last few years and is a relatively safe place to live, claims a shocking new report.

Following the highly exciting struggle for the throne by Donald III, and the ensuing battles, banishments and overthrowings in 1093-1094, Donald's successor Duncan II was murdered for being unpopular. Donald again seized the throne. However his brother Edgar defeated him with the help of an army and Donald was blinded and imprisoned on Iona.

However things calmed down drastically during Edgar's reign, to the extent that he was known as Edgar the Peaceable. Edgar, the son of Malcolm III (old Bighead) and Queen Margaret, ruled fairly and well. He may have ceded the Western Isles - including Iona, the cradle of Christianity in Scotland - to the Norwegians, but there have been no major wars for several years. Even relations with England are relatively cordial.

His successor and brother, Alexander, has continued this trend. Despite the promising nickname of Alexander the Fierce, he has spent much of his time encouraging monastic settlements and founding Inchcolm Abbey.

How can Scotland cope without wars, rebellions and struggles for the throne?

How can our fatalistic national character be maintained if there is peace and prosperity?

We need another hopeless war and we need one now!

Kings Dying of Natural Causes, says Another Shock Report

How Can This Be Happening in Scotland?

THE SHOCK REPORT, published today, reveals that the number of kings being dramatically murdered has SLUMPED since 1097, confirming a damning report of 1107.

For centuries, assassination or death in battle has been a traditional occupational hazard for Scottish kings, as our handy at-a-glance list shows:

- **Malcolm I: killed in a battle with the men of Moray in 950**
- **Indulf: killed in 962**
- **Duff: slain in Forres by the men of Moray in 967**
- **Culen: killed by the Britons in Lothian in 971**
- **Kenneth II: poisoned in 995 by Finella, whose son he had slain**
- **Constantine III: murdered in 997**
- **Kenneth III: slain in 1005 by Malcolm II**
- **Malcolm II: killed in 1034**
- **Duncan: slain in battle by Macbeth in 1040**
- **Macbeth: killed at Lumphanan in 1057 by Duncan's son, Malcolm Canmore**
- **Malcolm Canmore: treacherously murdered in 1093**

Since then however, Scotland has been governed by a string of kings who don't know the meaning of the phrase 'dramatic death'.

The rot set in with Donald III who was not murdered, merely blinded and imprisoned on Iona.

Edgar the Peaceable ruled well and was succeeded by his brother Alexander 'the Fierce'. Not fierce enough to die horribly apparently. Alexander passed the throne to his brother David I who - far from dying in battle or being bloodily slaughtered - died at his prayers in Carlisle Castle.

Malcolm the Maiden ('Maiden', I ask you!) and William the Lyon also died of natural causes.

Alexander II died on Kerrera without an assassin or enemy in sight.

Before you know it, they will be throwing themselves off cliffs to avoid violent deaths.

Traditionalists are mourning the apparent loss of the fine old Scots custom of gruesome Royal deaths.

Key Fact

The scholar and philosopher John of Duns - or Duns Scotus - gives the word Dunce to the Scots language.

Alexander in Death Plunge

Kingdom Set To Follow

KING ALEXANDER III of Scots has been thrown from his horse and killed, it was announced today. The King had been attending a council in Edinburgh Castle where it is understood he was discussing a Scottish earl being held by the English, and how his release might be brought about. The King was eager to be with his new young wife and set off to the ferry across the River Forth. The day had already seen some snowfalls and a high wind was up. At the Forth, the ferryman tried to dissuade the king from making the crossing as the wind and waves were rising. The King insisted, and the royal party made the crossing safely although on the other side of the Forth he was offered safe lodgings and urged to go no further that night.

The sequence of events is unclear, but it seems the king was riding ahead of his men and, in the darkness on the cliffs near Kinghorn, his horse stumbled and the king was thrown down a precipice to his death.

Our sources at Edinburgh Castle tell us that after the discussions of the day, the king and his lords dined on lamprey and wine and it is thought that this, together with his recklessness in riding ahead of his men, contributed to the tragedy.

Conspiracy theorists have already suggested that Edward I of England has some hand in the death of Alexander. The line of succession is troubled by the fact that both of the Scottish king's sons are dead. His only daughter, married to the King of Norway, died in childbirth, leaving her baby daughter Margaret - the 'Maid of Norway' - the heir to the Scottish throne, as she is Alexander's grandchild. Talks are already underway to bring Margaret to Scotland, but the current situation represents an opportunity for other nobles to make a claim for the throne, or for Edward to annex Scotland in its current state of confusion.

A court official, who wished to remain anonymous, told us:

'It was a damned English plot! And I've never liked lampreys. Actually, what the hell are lampreys?'

English Have Tails Shock!

IT'S TRUE! For a long time many north of the Border, indeed throughout the whole of Europe, have believed. But now we can reveal the shocking truth: the English have tails!

The revelation came following in-depth investigations by our dedicated team of slatterns.

Tavern-girl Tania told this paper today: 'Well, we were just getting down to it. I told him to remove his clothing. For a while all was well as he faced me. But then he turned around. I couldn't believe it. He had a tail! All curly and hairy. I was shocked. And the swine wouldn't pay me just because I threw up. He was probably English.'

Many theories have been put forward as to the origin of this strange mutation. Our Irish cousins suggest it may be because the English are the illegitimate offspring of the Welsh and sheep.

When we contacted the English Ambassador in Edinburgh he scowled, but his only comment was: 'You'll be sorry!'

How we laughed!

Maid of Norway Dies

Scotland Leaderless
Civil War Threatens

THE THREE-YEAR-OLD HEIR to the throne, Margaret, the Maid of Norway, has died en route to Scotland. Margaret - granddaughter of Alexander III, who died in 1286 - was the only direct heir to the throne. Her death destabilises all plans for a peaceful solution to Scotland's dynastic problems.

The Maid was crossing from Norway to assume the throne when she died. Reports are confused and it is not certain whether she was on board ship or on Orkney when she died.

Sources close to the throne warn that civil war is now a real possibility. The death of the Maid of Norway leaves a power vacuum which is likely to be hotly contested. The two most prominent candidates are Robert Bruce, Lord of Annandale, and John Balliol, Lord of Galloway and Barnard Castle. Outsiders include the kings of both England and Norway.

Key Fact

A power vacuum is a bit like a Dyson, but the suction isn't so strong.

Edward of England Declares Himself Overlord of Scotland

EDWARD I OF ENGLAND, great-uncle of the late Maid of Norway and a claimant to the throne of Scotland, has demanded the loyalty of the Scottish nobility.

In the turmoil over the succession which followed the death of the Maid of Norway, Edward had pledged to help Scotland's leaders at this difficult time. In addition, he has volunteered to judge the succession himself. However, it now emerges that he has requested the nobility acknowledge him as overlord of Scotland. Fearful of Edward's ambitions, and the possibility that he might seek to take advantage of the power vacuum north of the border, the nobles have refused.

The contestants for the Crown, however, are not prepared to jeopardise their claim to the throne. If they do not pledge their loyalty to Edward they exclude themselves from the succession. The strong claimant to the Crown, Robert Bruce has already sworn fealty to Edward, and it is thought that John Balliol, who may have the best case, will soon follow suit.

Key Fact

Power vacuums help nobles to suck up to their overlords and kings to clean up north of the border.

Lost and Found

Lost: Stone of Scone, 1296 or thereabouts. It looks a bit like a sewer cover but of great sentimental value. Needed to crown kings

Sting in the Tail

English Invade Scotland

John Balliol Deposed

Berwick Devastated, Thousands Feared Dead

The English have attacked the south of Scotland despite years of relative piece. A large southern army under Edward I has captured Berwick, slaughtering many of its inhabitants: old men, pregnant women, suckling babes and bright-eyed children. Nobody was spared! The shame of it!

The English forces marched north and met the gallant Scottish army near Dunbar. Our brave garrison at Dunbar Castle taunted the English, shouting: 'Tailed dogs – we will cut your tails off!'. The English appeared quite irritated. That showed them!

Our army, its recruits made up of men more used to farming and peaceful pursuits such as crochet and needlework, was - alas - cut to pieces by the barbaric and war-like English. And the garrison of the castle quickly surrendered. The shame of it!

The whole of Scotland is now laid open to the raping English, our nobles divided by their petty self interests, our ancient kingdom at the mercy of the Southron dogs. The shame of it!

Who can save us from English tyranny?

ADVERT
Clutter Your Living Room With

The Musical
Stone of Destiny Coffee Table

**For the first time - the symbol of Scotland's spirit,
recreated in finest quality plastic**

Branklyn Mint in Perth presents a musical collector's edition **Stone of Destiny Coffee Table**, lovingly recreated from a fuzzy picture postcard. Its turbulent history dates back to Biblical times when it was Jacob's Pillow. It belonged to the king, Fergus MacErc, who probably used it as a cesspit cover. For centuries it sat beneath the Coronation Chair at Scone, where the kings of Scots were inaugurated (sometimes in very quick succession). It was stolen and taken to Westminster Abbey by Edward I but was returned to Scotland in 1996. This is not such a grand gesture as it might appear: the stone is not worth any money, as it is too recognisable to sell, and it has no practical use whatsoever beyond propping doors open.

Now Branklyn Mint brings you your very own Stone of Destiny - yours to own and own again

Roughly actual size, the **Musical Stone of Destiny Coffee Table** has all these uses and more:

- Supporting magazines
- Holding up plates of scones and cups of tea
- Carrying your cans while watching TV
- Keeping your fish supper off the floor
- Or, put your feet up on it for a Royal rest

Ideal for Weddings!
Plays a variety of traditional Scottish tunes including *Flowers of the Forest*, *Letter from America* and *Spanish Eyes*

ORDER FORM
Post to:
Branklyn Mint, PO Box 100, Riverside Lockup Garages, Perth

Yes, I still haven't learned. Please send me the latest bit of tat, designed to appeal to my national pride and make me walk a little taller despite Scotland's near-Third World status. I enclose my credit card details. Oh, and there are loads of fivers in a jar by the bed.

Name _____ Address _____

_____ Postcode _____

YOUR GUARANTEE
*If you are not entirely satisfied with your Musical Stone of Destiny Coffee Table,
please let us know so we can do a moonlight flit.*

Secret Shame of William Wallace

RECENTLY UNCOVERED English court documents state that, on 8 August 1296, one Matthew of York, in the company of 'a thief, one William le Waleys' stole three shillings' worth of beer from a woman in Perth. Matthew, a cleric, was sentenced to do penance for his crime; his co-accused remained free. It is claimed that this is the young William Wallace, who knew this area well and was at this time living on his wits as a fugitive and an outlaw due to his reluctance to swear fealty to Edward I.

Certainly Wallace's career has not been without controversy. Tales of his courage and daring are legendary, including stories that he:

KILLED three English soldiers who tried to steal his catch while fishing

ELUDED English troops by disguising himself as a serving-maid, spinning by the fire while they searched the house

EVADED imprisonment by feigning death and having his body rescued from jail by his old nurse

MURDERED William Heselrig, the Sheriff of Lanark, in his bed after the Sheriff's execution of Wallace's wife, Marion Braidfoot, for abetting Wallace

SKINNED one knight and used his remains for a saddle bag

SLAUGHTERED scores of schoolboys in Corbridge

DEVASTATED Northumberland, robbing churches and harrying priests

STOLE sweets from a young child

His PR consultant, Henry the Minstrel, told us: 'There is no truth in these rumours at all. The similarity between the names of this thief, and that of William Wallace, Scotland's hero, is a complete coincidence.'

Henry the Minstrel is also known as 'Blind Harry', smells strongly of whisky and his stories may be completely without foundation.

Community Notice Board
Volunteers Wanted

William Wallace is raising an army to engage the forces of Edward I and assert Scotland's independence now that John Balliol has been tossed off the throne. If you can spare a few years of your free time, and are willing to die for your nation, why not volunteer? You must like travel and fighting, and hate the English.

Contact William Wallace, c/o Stirling Bridge.

William Wallace Heirloom Edition Collectible Bear

William Wallace. A legendary name in Scottish history and a tireless campaigner for Scottish independence. Now immortalised in the **William Wallace Heirloom Edition Collectible Bear.**

Wallace's efforts in the winter of 1297-8 drove the English almost totally out of Scotland. Now you can fight the good fight in your own home with this high-quality bear. With tartan sash, loveable furry ears and blue face, he captures all of Wallace's dignity and magnetism.

Commemorate His Bravery
Hang, Draw and Quarter William Wallace in your own home! This Collectible Bear comes with a finest quality miniature gibbet with silk cord and features detachable entrails in realistic catgut. Best of all, he easily splits into furry quarters for sending to the four corners of your kingdom.
Coming Soon
The Calgacus, Chief of Caledonii Collectible Bear

About the Artist
Morag Bean was brought up in a cave in Galloway and started her career robbing and eating passing travellers. She developed an interest in soft toys when she began to make crude effigies out of human skin. She has now risen to the top of her profession as a maker of fine quality collectible bears, shaped like famous Scots.

Order Form
I am a misty-eyed sentimentalist who thinks that the English ruined Scotland, and that until they arrived Scotland's splendour rivalled that of the Roman Empire, despite all the evidence to the contrary. Please send me the William Wallace Bear so it can join the other tartan tat and Bowling Club trophies on my mantelpiece.

Name _____

Address _____

*Certificate
of Authenticity*
This is an authentic Morag Bean Heirloom Edition Collectible Bear.
Please note our use of the word 'collectible' does not guarantee it is worth the money you pay for it. Nor does the word 'heirloom' guarantee that your descendants will thank you for it.

SCOTLAND IN DESPAIR
WALLACE GUTTED!

**There are those who say the execution of William
Wallace was over the top.**

*They say that dragging him through the streets was unnecessary.
That it went too far to emasculate him and burn his intestines before
his very eyes. That there was no need to behead him. And that
sending the quarters of his body to the four corners of his kingdom
was just showing off.*

Come off it, Jock-fanciers! You may be in despair, but
we English are far from gutted!

**If Wallace hadn't been defeated by the English at the Battle of
Falkirk, he would be quietly retired by now. Or a farmer.**

These face-painting barbarians have to know their place.

And in a free country it is our God-given right to say so.

And we don't have tails!

Pub Fight Decides
King of Scots

**ROBERT BRUCE announced himself
King of Scots after a pub fight.**

That's the claim of controversial
Scottish historian Dr Ceilidh Minogue.
Dr Minogue claims to have unearthed
papers which show fierce rivals Bruce
and Red Comyn, so called because of his
red hair, had met to discuss their right
to the throne. Both had claimed to be
the true King of Scotland in the past and
violent arguments had flared between
them. The two had decided to meet in
Greyfriars Pub to discuss the future of
Scotland. A fight broke out and Red
Comyn was killed by Bruce.

Dr Minogue says: 'I have uncovered
documents which say the altercation
came about as the result of a spilt pint
but accounts differ. One minute they
were rowing at the fruit machine, the
next Red Comyn was on the floor. My
view is this. I believe Bruce said
something about 'never hold the
cherries' and then it was all over.'

Key Fact

The fight in question was not in
Greyfriars Pub but Greyfriars Church in
Dumfries. Being guilty of murder and
sacrilege, Bruce went into hiding. By
1307, however, he had won several
victories and began to push the English
out of Scotland.

Eddie's Fingers Bannockburned!

Edward Hammered by the Scots!

'Come on if you think you're hard enough.' That was our challenge to Edward II! He did and we gave him a damn good thrashing. The English king had to crawl away with his tail between his legs. He won't be coming back up to Scotland in a hurry.

You got hammered! And what's more we get to keep all the plunder. Loads of cash! This lot will fetch plenty of money on the open market and your favourite paper has managed to get hold of some rare pieces of plunder. If you complete the following sentence and send it in, you could have your own bit of valuable hardware:

'The last place I'd want a red-hot poker is ...'

Military Disaster

THE HUMILIATION at Bannockburn was a sorry failure and characteristic of Edward II's military adventures. He has neither the ruthlessness of his father nor the intelligence and guile of his son. It is particularly impressive as it is rare for an English army to suffer a defeat and this is a big one! More English knights were slain and captured at Bannockburn than at any other battle.

So why? Partly the English were over-confident. Their army was far bigger than the Scottish force but truth is that the defeat came by virtue of superior tactics. Robert the Bruce fought a canny battle. He had chosen his ground well. The much larger number of troops on the English side was nullified by the narrow front that they could actually fight on. When they couldn't break through the battle squares of spearmen, the English foot soldiers were driven back into the burn where they were slaughtered.

On the first day of the battle the English horsemen almost broke through and captured Bruce – although the English knight Henry de Bohun had his head cleaved by Bruce in the melee – that was their only success and when they failed, they set the stage for a dramatic Scottish victory. The usual blood-curdling charge of the Scots, which led them into so many defeats, was controlled until the battle had been won.

Despite the decisiveness of this victory it will take another 14 years and a new king, Edward III, before England offers peace with the Treaty of Edinburgh.

How Did Bannockburn Get Its Name?

by Dr Ceilidh Minogue

AS EVERY HISTORIAN KNOWS, Bannockburn is quite near Stirling Castle, and the stream known as the Bannock Burn flows into the River Forth about four miles east of the castle. But how did it get its unusual name? Recent research suggests that the stream was originally known locally simply as 'the Burn'.

In July 1314, the English king Edward II was on his way to engage the forces of Robert the Bruce when he passed a bannock factory near Stirling. Knowing bannocks – a sort of oatmeal biscuit – were the Bruce's favourite food (and handy to put in a packed lunch [a lunch which is packed in such a way as to both be portable and tasty] on the battlefield) the ruthless Edward ordered the factory blown up. The explosion sent bannocks flying for miles around and the bulk of them fell into the burn, which literally ran with bannocks. Amazed locals immediately named it 'Bannock Burn' and gathered handfuls of the delicacy. However, the bannocks were too wet to eat, as were the locals.

Key Fact

Burn is the Scottish name for a stream or small river. Why it was called Bannock is anyone's guess. And why those gritty little biscuits (which resemble coasters) are called 'bannocks' is also lost in the mists of time.

The Daily Rock

Edinburgh's liveliest pamphlet!!

Come-on Pope! Recognise us as a proper country and tell those buggers down in England to do the same!

See inside for our maiden of the day.

Win a pair of wooden teeth just like the Lord Advocate's

Dear Pope ...

Declaration of Arbroath Asserts Scottish Freedom

'SO YOU'VE WRITTEN to the Pope then Tam?'

'Aye.'

'The whole thing is in Latin, why's that?'

'Well, he's the Pope, you've got to show a bit of respect.'

'So Tam tell us, this Declaration of Arbroath, what's it all about?'

'I'm glad you asked me that. Basically we're wanting him to OK Bruce, Robert the Bruce that is!'

'There's a bit in it that says you're prepared to fight until there are just a 100 of you alive?'

'Aye.'

'What then?'

'Well hopefully I'll be one of those and personally I intend to take up something quiet, needlework or cheese making in a little out of the way country until all the fuss dies down.'

Key Fact

The Declaration of Arbroath was a letter dated 6 April 1320 to the Pope. It was sealed by the senior nobles in Scotland. Pope John XXII, unlike his predecessors, hadn't accepted Scottish Independence and had supported the claims of Edward I that Scotland was merely a part of the English kingdom. This was an attempt to answer the English propaganda with a firm assertion of Scottish rights and the legitimacy of the King, Robert I, The Bruce.

Often quoted is the following passage: 'Yet even if the same Robert, should he turn aside from the task and yield Scotland or us to the English king or people, him we should cast out as the enemy of us all, and choose another king to defend our freedom; for so long as a hundred of us remain alive, we will yield in no least way to English dominion. For we fight, not for glory nor for riches nor for honour, but only and alone for freedom, which no good man surrenders but with his life.'

It should be said that nobody paid much attention to this last part...

Spider Loses Claim Against King

SHAPELY ARACHNID Ms Spider, 19, today lost her court case against Robert the Bruce, King of Scots. As Ms Spider scuttled from court in a flood of tears, a spokesperson for Bruce claimed that he felt no ill will towards his former companion. 'It is true that they shared some time together in a cave,' said the spokesperson, 'but there never was any commitment between them. The idea that Ms Spider inspired King Robert to try again and take the throne, that without her he would have remained nothing but an excommunicated treacherous outlaw with few followers, is just preposterous.'

Meanwhile Ms Spider was inconsolable. From her cave in Arran she issued the following statement: 'I just cannot believe he could do this to me. When we met he was depressed and despairing. His kingdom was in ruins. It was my perseverance and determination that saw him through. I was his inspiration. Now he is King of Scots, and I am still an ordinary spider lass with a half-finished web and hundreds of pupae nearing gestation.'

In a separate development King Robert has also denied having anything to do with Ms Spider's 243 offspring. 'Ms Spider is clearly very upset,' said a spokesman, 'but this claim is simply a web of lies.'

Key Fact

Bruce's daughter Marjory was married to Walter FitzAlan, Hereditary Steward of Scotland. He was known as Walter Steward and the founders of what became the Stewart dynasty after David II, Bruce's son, had no heirs.
Plenty of troubles followed this!

LOST and FOUND
Lost: heart. Last seen heading towards Spain. If found return to Scotland. Contact Dunfermline Abbey or the estate of Robert the Bruce. If it can't be buried with the rest of him, stick it in Melrose Abbey with the Douglases.

Obituary
Robert the Bruce, King of Scots

It was 1306 when Robert the Bruce murdered the Red Comyn and then set himself up on the throne. He was promptly excommunicated by the church and then faced the retribution of Edward I.

Things didn't immediately go all that well. He lost a battle at Methven and in the following months three of his brothers were executed, his wife, child and sisters captured, and Bruce was a hunted fugitive.

But then the tide turned in 1307. Bruce won the battle of Loudoun Hill in May, and by July Edward I was dead!

From the following battles on Scottish soil, and despite all the death and destruction, there came a realisation, in both Scotland and England, that Scotland was actually an independent nation and not just another part of northern England.

This was a time of success for Scotland militarily. Coincidentally the same period saw the foppish Edward II on the English throne. He managed to lead England to defeat at both Bannockburn and later the Battle of Byland. In comparison to his ruthless father, Edward I, and to his son Edward III, he was indecisive and vacillating. He was not, by any standards, either a good soldier or a successful king. He was also facing in Bruce a general who knew when to fight and when not to.

Robert the Bruce was leading Scotland to victory but he was also creating a sense of nationhood. He realised that the feudal system, where people owed their loyalty to the local lord or baron, would not sustain Scotland and there needed to be a bigger entity to which loyalty was to be pledged.

The Declaration of Arbroath in 1320, although it didn't immediately gain Scotland recognition as an independent state, was another step on the way.

Edward III finally recognised Scotland's independence in 1328-9. This was a year before Robert the Bruce died, which may have been a comfort to him as he succumbed to which is believed to have been leprosy, although probably not.

So a reign that started with murder ended with a country.

Key Fact

Are you a king? Thinking of building a castle and garrisoning it? Then read this and you might think again.

The average castle designed to protect your borders and ensure that you can keep collecting your income is now costing up to £12,000. For Edward III of England that is a tenth of his income, so that would be Scotland twenty times over. 'I'm also being charged an outrageous ten grand to pay my troops and make sure they are fed and kitted out.'

Own Goal
Dupplin Moor Disaster: Scots Army Crushed

'Well Tommy, a lot of critics would say that reverting to the discredited mounted knight attack Scotland played into English hands.'

'No, I think we were fighting to our strengths. We had a lot of lads on horses and plenty of armour in the changing room. On the day we did what should have been done.'

'But you lost!'

'Aye well, it's alright to criticise Scotland with hindsight. We came into this one showing great form on the back of Bannockburn but we went to pieces down the middle.'

'It would be fair to say that your flanks weren't very strong either.'

'I think it was more the English were strong, rather than we were weak!'

'The ground seemed a bit rough, Tommy?'

'Terrible, Archie, just terrible. If you're going to have a decent battle you've got have a decent fighting surface.'

'So where now?'

'Well, there was the friendly at Halidon.'

'Er, you lost that too.'

'Well the English have offered us a replay at Neville's Cross in 1346, I like our chances there so we'll be taking them up on it.'

'I suspect it will be another disaster if you don't change your tactics. But good luck. Any hints about your team?'

'The key word I think will be chivalry! Our chairman (King David II, son of Robert the Bruce) is very keen on it!'

Own Goal
Neville's Cross Disaster: Scots Army Crushed

'Well Tommy, a lot of critics would say' etc...

Proof that Scots Eat Carrots
Scots Win Battle of Otterburn

THE NEW TACTICS introduced by James Douglas, 2nd Earl of Douglas, have paid off handsomely. Getting into a bit of stramash with Henry Percy, inventor of the Hotspur comic, Douglas chose to fight at night. A brilliant plan, which sadly he wasn't able to see through to the conclusion.

By choosing to actually fight rather than direct from a safe distance Douglas got a nasty graze, which he soon realised was a fatal stab wound. Aware that it would probably demoralise his soldiers and embolden the enemies he instructed that he be hidden in the undergrowth. When Percy realised that defeat was inevitable he offered to surrender to the Scots leader. The Scottish knights told him to surrender to a bush. They were then able to claim that the battle had been won by a dead man.

History Just Too Boring to Record

IT IS HARD to believe but in just 30 short years history has become boring.

A leading academic told us: 'It's true. When William Wallace and Robert the Bruce were doing their stuff, there was plenty of material to interest us: wars, campaigns, politics, foreign involvement, disembowelments. Now things are just dull. True, fighting goes on. But, hey, who cares? It's just so boring. Even the kings are dull, so dull they can't even be bothered thinking up new names. Two more Roberts and four or five Jameses.

'By the middle of the sixteenth century you are into the Reformation. Now James IV was starting to become interesting, what with his love of enormous cannons and warships. James V was a bit boring, but then you have Mary, Queen of Scots. She was a woman so you have feminist issues, there was the Reformation so you have religious issues, there was the relationship between monarch and people, there is just so much to write about. It's great.'

'But the 15th century? Just too dull.'

Own Goal
Homildon Hill Disaster
Return to Old Tactics: Scots Army Crushed

'Well Tommy, a lot of critics would say' etc...

Horoscopes

James I 1406-37

Looks like you'll be in for a long visit in London. Try to get out and see the place if you can. Perth is an unlucky place for you. 1437 will not be a good year.

Obituary

James was held for 18 years in London, after being captured aboard ship, mostly in the Tower. He was murdered by Sir Robert Graham in Perth. The reasons were partly because the lead conspirator the Earl of Atholl had a claim to the throne and partly because the king was very greedy passing a lot of laws to satisfy his financial needs.

James II 1437-60

Investing in cannon futures would be good long term planning but watch out that this policy doesn't backfire.

Obituary

James II went a long way to creating a consolidated kingdom. He took the advice of James Kennedy, Archbishop of St Andrews, and picked off his enemies one by one. Met his end attacking Roxburgh Castle where a cannon exploded and killed him.

James III 1460-88

Think twice before you trust people. By that we mean everyone, yes everyone especially relations. Watch your back, especially when your relatives are about! Brothers, cousins, children.

Other people to watch out for are Dukes, Lords, the English and did we mention children?

Obituary

Living a long life was always tricky for a king. James III survived a number of major upheavals but then came up against an army under the command of his fifteen-year-old son at Sauchieburn.

The king lost and was killed during his escape, fulfilling the prophecy that he would be betrayed by his nearest kin.

James IV 1488-1513

Ships will play a big role in your thinking, but don't overestimate their importance. Treaties will be important too, so try to make sure you don't break yours. Don't get involved in any battles you might get hurt, or die. Probably the latter.

Obituary

Regarded by many as a successful king, he certainly went further down the route of creating one kingdom out of the warring lands north of the border. However after a long peace with England he got drawn into inter-European squabbles on the French side. A major miscalculation saw him crossing the English Border. The result was the major defeat of Flodden where the king was killed. An unnecessary battle, in a cause that wasn't Scotland's, and over issues which had already been resolved by the French and English.

A Day In The Life Of A Big Boat

PEOPLE OFTEN saw me sailing along and would remark in wonder: 'what a big boat!' And I am that, the Great Michael. It's said that it took all the wood in Fife to make me and I can carry over 1,400 people on board. King James IV built lots of ships but I was his favourite. Sadly my history is not covered in as much glory as I would have wished.

There was a shortage of skilled men such as gunners and sailors in Scotland so I was never going to work to full capacity. Because there were so many people on board, you can imagine what it was like to be stuck on a ship like me. Oh, the conditions were terribly insanitary and disease and infections spread quickly throughout my crew and the soldiers. I was at the cutting edge but because I was so big I was a bit of pig to steer.

I think, really, I was just a status symbol and because I was so big and so expensive I made James IV feel like a real king!

But it was a difficult time. In 1512 War broke out. The members of the 'Holy League', Spain, Venice and latterly England set themselves against the French presence in Italy.

Belligerently, my owner, James entered on the French side. You know, I personally think it was more as a way of getting at Henry VIII his brother-in-law, rather than because he wanted to support any French claims. I was loaned to the French along with the Scottish fleet and because of all my cannons, all his best gunners went with me. I heard that this caused a problem later.

But once I got there, what were the French like? Actually they really made little use of me and even allowed me to run aground, typical isn't it? That was about it for me. James went off to some place called Flodden, but he never wrote and I never heard from him again.

It's a Flodden Disaster

Scots defeated by the English at Flodden

DISASTER HAS struck at the heart of Scotland. James IV is dead. The army has been destroyed. Outnumbered our brave soldiers fought courageously. The odds were overwhelming and true to their nature the English devils with no sense of civility slaughtered poor innocent and peaceful Scots.

'We were just doing a bit of shopping in Northumberland when we realised that a big gang of thugs was out looking for trouble,' said David, 26, from Drumelzier. 'We didn't want to get involved so we headed back home. But they caught up with us at Branxton Hill,

it was just awful, they were like wild animals and they just attacked anyone who was carrying a sword, hagbut, musket, armour or spear.

'I only got away by hiding in the slurry,' he told us from a distance.

We Say ...
It was an unprovoked attack by the cowardly English!

Ooooh it makes us mad! Surely free Scots should be allowed to have a day out in England without being molested and our king slaughtered.

Yes, we were mates with the French, so what!

First Leader on Flodden

PART OF THE REASON for this massive defeat was that most of the best gunners were all on our ship, the Great Michael. They were providing support for the French against the Holy League. What were they doing there when they could have been with the rest of our army where it mattered?

In July 1513 the remaining cream of the Scottish soldiers marched on England. As this was a proper army, not just a rough and ready rabble, as usual, we must also consider the theory that James IV was not a great soldier. We should not speak ill of the dead but it has been said of him that he acted before he'd made his mind up. So it was probably unfortunate that the man he came up against, Thomas Howard Earl of Surrey, was a professional soldier battle hardened and strategically aware.

Surrey manoeuvred his troops at Flodden so that the English force was between our Scots army and

the way back home. Then the Scottish army was crushed.

This has been a disaster on a massive scale. Wherever you look in Scotland you can see how it has affected everyone. It's fair to say that the whole country has been stunned by this. Our force was well armed, well disciplined and motivated for victory. But it has been completely destroyed, and our king was killed together with thirteen earls, the dean of Glasgow, the provost of Edinburgh and thousands of our brave young men. What is so hard to bear is that this defeat was to the second string and smaller English force.

This paper suggests that it will have major repercussions in the long term for Europe. Here in Scotland we have been shell-shocked by this defeat, and we should no longer be prepared to embark on campaigns to support the French. It is time to draw in our horns and think of Scotland.

Horoscope

James V 1513-1542

You will be fond of children. You won't be quite so fond of marrying their mothers. Your 30th year is unlikely to be lucky. Think about being nice to religious leaders as you never know when that's going to pay off.

Obituary

James had many illegitimate children, and even some in wedlock, but only Mary (who had just been born when James died) of the legitimate children has survived, prompting that old inaccurate saying 'It cam with a lass and it'll gang with a lass'. James's talent for sucking up to the pope paid dividends when he was granted a permanent tax of £10,000 from the Scottish prelacies and a temporary tax equal to a tenth of the income of all Scottish ecclesiastical revenues.

Own Goal

Battle of Solway Moss Disaster

'Well Tommy, a lot of critics would say' etc...

James V, in overall command of the troops, said after the battle: 'Woe is me. We have done so badly I just wish I was dead.'

So, he tootled north to Falkland, and died.

Battle of the Shirts

The Daily Fraser

What a bunch of Nancy Boys!

WE TRASHED THE CLANS RANALD and won a great victory today at the Great Glen. Vastly outnumbered, our defiant clansman fought the wicked and (it has to be said rather effeminate) Clans Ranald. We spoke to our four victorious survivors.

'Well that taught the bastards a lesson they won't forget in a hurry. They won't be so eager to ambush us in the future.'

How do you account for this great triumph?

'They're just a bunch of pansies. There must have been over 700 of them at the start but there couldn't have been more than eight of them left at the end.'

The Evening Ranald

Frasers Erasered!

NEWS JUST IN OF A TREMENDOUS VICTORY over the Clan Fraser. Proving to the world they are as stupid as they look, they took on the Clans Ranald and got a real kicking for their trouble.

A real triumph for us all to savour over a clan well known for their aversion to soap and water.

We talked to the eight victors.

'It was tough but in the end we stuffed them!'

'The dirty soap dodgers didn't stand a chance, to be honest we were more worried about getting a sunburn than fighting them.'

This dispute was apparently over the chieftainship of the Clan Donald of Moidart, which both clans claimed. Whatever the reason, on a day so hot that the combatants fought in their shirts, they fought a battle so ferocious that out of some 1,100 who started only 12 were left at the end. It also achieved staggeringly little except that the Clans Ranald got a visit from the Earl of Huntly and his troops on behalf of James V.
It makes you wonder why they fought to so bitter an end.

Own Goal
Pinkie Disaster
'Well Tommy, a lot of critics etc'

Calvin Declines

'Not for us!' said French hardman John Calvin when asked about Catholicism.

'You've got to know that man is totally powerless before God. God is omnipotent. Everything in this world is planned. It's what's called 'predestination'. The good thing, well for us Calvinists, is that we're God's elect. Sometimes we may fail him but that doesn't matter now, because he's already handed out our tickets to an eternally pleasurable afterlife.'

HOLYROOD NIGHTS
The latest celebrity gossip
Big news in Holyrood is that sex bomb Mary Queen of Scots' love life is in trouble again. Mary, in France for an extended holiday and shopping trip, dated the Dauphin and insiders said romance was in the air... They married, he died and she returned to Scotland and married again on the rebound. Eligible bachelor Henry Stewart, Lord Darnley, became the second Mr MQS but before long she was seen around town with pint-sized chart-topping Italian sex thimble David Rizzio and insiders said romance was in the air... The 'just good friends' pair caused so much gossip that jealous Darnley stabbed Rizzio to death. And guess what? Unlucky in love Mary lost her second husband when Darnley was blown up at top night-spot Kirk o' Field. Word is she's been swept off her feet by hot Scot James Hepburn, Earl of Bothwell. Insiders say romance is in the air...

OPPORTUNITY KNOX

OLD ENEMIES John Knox and Mary, Queen of Scots have been at loggerheads again.

A press release issued today by the Palace states that the Queen, 24, merely wishes to practice Roman Catholic mass in her private chapel. The mass - outlawed by the Scottish Parliament in 1561 - is important to the Queen due to her Catholic upbringing in France. But staunch Protestant and Terror of the Reformation John Knox (45, 52 or 56, depending on who you believe) is having none of it.

'One mass is more terrible to me than 10,000 armed invaders,' declared the Father of Presbyterianism yesterday. 'The Church of Rome is the Synagogue of Satan! The Catholic clergy of Scotland are gluttons, wantons and licentious revellers, but who yet regularly and meekly partake of the sacrament.'

The Queen is said to be furious at the attitude of the bearded Godbotherer. However, grudge-bearing Knox - known as the 'Thundering Scot' for his impressive orations from the Pulpit of St Giles Cathedral - has accused the Monarch of:

TRYING to bribe him with political power
LIVING a life of flirtation and suspected adulteries
BLUBBING when he shouts at her

The Queen has reportedly said 'I fear the prayers of John Knox more than all the assembled armies of Europe.'

Hulloo! Magazine presents
AT HOME WITH JOHN KNOX

The Terror of the Reformation Shows Us Round His Gracious Home Which He Decorated Himself

The Father of Presbyterianism Tells Us
His Hopes – His Fears – His Plans for the Future

The 'Thundering Scot' Shares His Private Self In A Hulloo! Exclusive

As his servant ushers me into a low-ceilinged hallway decorated in a traditional 'medieval grim' style and shows me to a charming rough wooden bench, I wonder about the respected and much feared orator I am about to meet. When he enters, he is surprisingly small; not at all the impressive and thundering figure he presents in the pulpit of St Giles Kirk. I am reminded of the words of Thomas Smeaton, who said, 'I know not if God ever placed a more godly and great spirit in a body so little and frail. I am certain, that there can scarcely be found another in whom more gifts of the Holy Ghost, for the comfort of the Church of Scotland, did shine.'

HULLOO!: Now let's start at the beginning. You were born in 1505 –

JK: 1514.

HULLOO!: It says 1505 here. And 1508. When did you become a priest?

JK: I was ordained as a priest in the Roman Catholic Church when John Calvin began the Reformation of Geneva.

HULLOO!: You were a Roman Catholic. It's a bit of a turnaround to end up as one of the staunchest enemies of the Catholic Church, isn't it? How did that happen?

JK: George Wishart introduced me to the thinking of the Reformation. I was his bodyguard when he was preaching, to protect him from assassination attempts. But his mission set Catholic Scotland against him and he was burned at the stake by Cardinal Beaton. (*thundering tone*) From that hour I was the enemy of the Roman Catholic Church.

HULLOO!: And two years later, Beaton was assassinated by 'parties unknown'.

JK (*still thundering*): Are you suggesting something?!

HULLOO!: Er, no.

JK (*working up to full auto-rant*): I accused the Catholic clergy of Scotland of being gluttons, wantons and licentious revellers, but who yet regularly and meekly partook of the sacrament. I did preach to the exiled nobles who had killed Beaton; after I first preached, one of my listeners declared 'Others snipped at the branches of popery; but he strikes at the roots, to destroy the whole'.

HULLOO!: (*trying to change the subject*): What was your next career move?

JK (*calming slightly*): French troops captured our castle and I began nineteen months as a galley slave.

HULLOO!: And was there a lighter side to that?

JK: There was. A picture of the Virgin Mary was brought on board to be kissed by the slaves. When I refused, the picture was thrust into my face. (*going up a gear*) Outraged, I flung the accursed idol into the river, saying 'Let our Lady learn to swim!'

HULLOO!: Right... well, er, and has travel played a big part in your life?

JK: I was in wandering exile for thirteen years if that's what you mean. After the galley slave thing, I went to England for five years and became a royal chaplain. Along comes Mary Tudor to put a stop to that. Better a Marian exile than a Marian martyr, I thought, and I travelled to Frankfurt and Geneva to study under Calvin.

HULLOO!: And what made you come home?
JK: My fame as a preacher spread and I returned to Scotland to reform the country. During 1560 and 1561, I persuaded the Scottish Parliament to accept the reformed confession of faith.

HULLOO!: But there was one more problem wasn't there? Mary, Queen of Scots - brought up a Catholic in France.

JK (*grimly*): Soon after she came here, I met with her to bring her heart to Jesus. But no, she tries converting me back to Roman Catholicism with bribes of political power. I knew nothing good would come of it! Not for her, anyway; I'm laughing all the way to the next world.

HULLOO!: What do you remember most about her?

JK: She tried to restore the Roman mass in her private chapel - although Parliament had outlawed it. She lived a life of suspected adulteries. She married her second husband's presumed murderer, the Earl of Bothwell. Then she turns on the waterworks!

HULLOO!: She tried to win you over with womanly wiles?

JK: I was having none of it. I said at the time, one mass was more terrible to me than the landing of 10,000 armed invaders. I preached against the restoration of the church of Rome, which the 'Lords of the Congregation' - nobles who supported me - had termed the 'Synagogue of Satan'.

HULLOO!: What happened next to Mary next?

JK: She abdicated after being brought down by her own nobles. Serves her right. Execution's too good for her.

HULLOO!: Well at least you're not bitter.

JK: I don't want you to think I am. Let me give you a signed copy of my book. Between you and me, it's about Mary Queen of Scots.
HULLOO!: What's it called?
JK: The First Blast of the Trumpet Against the Monstrous Regimen of Women.
HULLOO!: Oh dear.

Book Review

The First Book of Discipline (1559)

My eyes lit up when I was asked to review the latest work from Johnny Knox. As a keen devotee of the arts of obedience and discipline, I was very pleased to give it a go. You can imagine my disappointment to discover that it was in a plain cover only because it was so serious. I understand from the first few pages (I didn't read the rest) that it is in fact a book to regulate the parishes. Yes, yes, I'm sure that there are many people who are interested in how to regulate parish revenues and make provision for the poor but I'm not one of them!

That one about the Monstrous Women was just as dull. When will the Marquis de Sade be born?

Key Fact

The form of the name 'Stuart' is from a French misspelling of 'Stewart' during the reign of Mary.

"My Beheading HELL"
by Mary, Queen of Scots
Exclusive for Hulloo! Magazine

We visit Mary, Queen of Scots at Fotheringay Castle as she awaits her execution
We discuss her life – her dreams – ~~her hopes for the future~~

HULLOO! *Magazine*: Mary's life has always known turmoil. She became queen upon the death of her father James V when she was just a week old. Henry VIII attempted to marry her to his son in an attempt to gain control of Scotland, a process now know as 'The Rough Wooing'. The betrothal was annulled by the Scottish parliament, and war with England followed. After the defeat of the Scots at the Battle of Pinkie, the infant Queen was sent to France for her own safety. As she enters the room for our interview I am struck by her height and her striking elegance. She seems more French than Scottish. And with her magnificent red hair, it is hard to believe that glamorous Mary is 44 years old.

HULLOO!: Mary, you were raised in France, is that right?

MQS: Correct. I married the Dauphin - later Francis II - in 1558 and on his death in 1560 I became dowager Queen of France, with my own estates and wealth.

HULLOO!: And you sparkled at the French court, I believe! Did you have lots of hobbies?

MQS: I excelled at hunting, dancing, and music, and I spoke and read six languages. If that's what you mean.

HULLOO!: How did you feel when you returned to Scotland from France?

MQS: It was very difficult. I barely remembered the country I had left as a child. In addition the death of my mother, Mary of Guise, had left the country in a fluid and volatile political state. The country was effectively run by the so-called Lords of the Congregation - who were all Protestants! So as a devout Catholic, I had my hands full.

HULLOO!: Did your Scottish subjects welcome you with open arms?

MQS: Not exactly. A Protestant riot threatened the first mass held in my private chapel at Holyrood. The Mass was banned by Parliament to all but myself and my immediate household.

HULLOO!: Was romance in the air at this point?

MQS: Who writes these questions? In 1565 I married my cousin, Henry Stewart, Lord Darnley.

HULLOO!: Childhood sweethearts, perhaps?

MQS: No. He was a grandson of Margaret Tudor and strengthened my claim to the English throne. However, it soon became clear that it wasn't going to work.

HULLOO!: Was there domestic discord?

MQS: He murdered my secretary David Rizzio in front of my eyes if that's the sort of thing you mean.

HULLOO!: So there's no chance of a reconciliation?

MQS: Hardly. He was killed when a house blew up at Kirk o' Field in 1567.

HULLOO!: I'll write down 'widowed in

tragic accident' shall I?

MQS: If you call being chased out of an exploding house and strangled naked in the yard an accident you can, yes.

HULLOO!: And did they ever identify the assassin?

MQS: There was quite a list, but the chief suspect was the Earl of Bothwell.

HULLOO!: And did you have him punished?

MQS: Well not exactly ... I made him Duke of Orkney. Er, and then I married him.

HULLOO!: I'll write 'found true love with a real man' then, will I?

MQS: You can if you like. Did you do any preparation for this interview?

HULLOO!: Well, I bought a new pen...

MQS: Anyway, that was my undoing. Bothwell (*spits*) was regarded as Darnley's murderer. I was constrained at Loch Leven by the most radical of the Protestant nobles, and made to sign an act of abdication in favour of my infant son who shortly became James VI.

HULLOO!: Well -

MQS: My infant son shortly became James VI. Shortly. Did you see what I did there?

HULLOO!: Your Majesty has an uncommon wit. Yes. What happened next?

MQS: After the defeat of my army at the Battle of Langside, I threw myself on the mercy of my cousin, Elizabeth I.

HULLOO!: And has she been good to you?

MQS: She's kept me prisoner for nineteen years in a variety of draughty old castles. I have been the focus of various ludicrous Catholic plots to raise me to the English throne and tomorrow morning Elizabeth is having me beheaded, so 'good' isn't the word I'd use.

HULLOO!: Well, I think that brings us up to date. Thank you for the interview. I'll have a transcript sent round tomorrow.

MQS: Chuck it in the basket, I'll read it after the execution.

A new confection ...
Calvinist Hearts

- Nae Dancin'
- Avoid the Demon Drink
- Burn In Hell
- Have Ye Sinned?
- Nae Guid Will Come o' This
- ..But We Pay For It

Horoscope

James VI 1567-1625

Think big when it comes to kingdoms. But remember Irish policies are likely to have long-term repercussions.

The Official Scottish History Doll Collectors Club

Mary, Queen of Scots

Recreate the execution of *Mary, Queen of Scots* in your own home with this strikingly realistic collectible doll. With superbly detailed costume and detachable head, this collector's item is a must for every true aficionado of Scottish history's grimmer moments. See for yourself the resignation of the spirit. Experience first hand the shrinking of the flesh. And splash on the tomato ketchup for added realism.

2001
441st Anniversary
Tenuous Cash-in
Heirloom Edition

Special Features

Mary, Queen of Scots comes complete with

* Lovingly crafted small dog to cower under skirts
* Realistic wig to slip off her severed head
* Certificate of authenticity in Old High Gaelic (may appear to resemble Chinese)

About the Artist

Chantelle Ogg has created some of the world's most popular collectible doll designs for The Official Scottish History Doll Collectors Club. In 1997 she won the prestigious Scottish Tourism Board Award for Export with her 'Exploding Henry Stewart, Lord Darnley'.

Coming soon:

* The Battle of Nechtansmere Chess Set
* The Death of James V Wall Clock
* The Massacre of Glencoe Egg-Timer
* The Highland Clearances Tea-Towel

Order Form

You can view the *Mary, Queen of Scots Doll* in your own home for seven days, so long as you give us your credit card number: _____

☐ I am an American silage consultant one more waffle away from a coronary and am under the mistaken belief that having a great-great-aunt from Ross and Cromarty makes me 'Scatch'. Please add me to your mailing list.

Dreams Do Come True

I'm King of England Now!

'IT'S A BIG DAY this for me,' said James VI as he leant over and pinched the cheek of his favourite, Robert Carr.

'Yesterday I was just king of a very draughty kingdom plagued with rough Highland folk and midges, with porridge for breakfast, lunch and dinner. Today I'm king of Britain. I'm rich now. I've got palaces and castles. I can live in London. You know if I have to go back to Scotland ever again that will be once too many. I will only go up there for something important: probably just to sort out the church.'

'I feel a genuine sense of release down here. Poverty is a thing of the past. Mary, my mother, almost ruined everything with her constant plotting against Queen Elizabeth. You know I'm sorry that she was executed, truly I am. But she did bring it on herself. If she hadn't antagonised the Queen like she did. Anyway, all's well that ends well and I'm king!'

'You know something, Robert. I can probably run Scotland from down here. I shall write and tell them what to do. None of my ancestors could rule Scotland with their armies and all that fighting but I probably can with this pen. Well any of my pens, not just this one. Actually I quite like that thought. I shall have to work it up into a quotation that I can leave to posterity.'

'One of the things I am going to sort out is the general lawlessness. For God's sake, they keep on raiding each other and killing each other. It's not good. Makes us look uncivilised: this is the 17th century now. Are the French always fighting each other and the Spanish? I'm going to stamp down on it - the MacGregors for starters and Earl Pate, cousin or not: they're both going to get a lesson in the strong arm of the King of Britain's law.'

Castle Building Reaches Epidemic Proportions

TIME WAS when only the richest nobility could afford a castle. But now with the parcelling out of church lands and the advent of the tower house every Tam, Dick and Harry can have their own fortress. Estimates have put the number of strongholds in Scotland at between 2700 and 3000.

'This is great,' said one commentator, 'not only does it give work to many masons, labourers and servants, but these buildings will be a great asset to the tourist industry in the centuries to come. Who knows, but it could be that in four hundred years people will still be making a living from castles. I predict a book, running to at least three editions.'

Back to the Loch Ness region today as my grandmother's family came from there in the 1890s and I really wanted to find the family castle. Found this place called Castle Urquhart and get this, the owner was working in the car park. When I told him I was looking for my family castle, he told me that until 1939, this place was known as Castle Weinstein, but they changed it because it sounded too German! Of all the castles in Scotland, I had stumbled across my ancestral home! And, for only fifty cents (they call them 'poonds' here) he even gave me a certificate to say I was entitled to inherit it when he died. I'll have you all to stay when I'm living in my castle!   Diana

Postcards from the Old Country
by Diana J. Weinstein III

Nessieburger and Chip Van, Urquhart by Loch Ness

COMMENT

When James VI succeeded Elizabeth I as ruler of England,
we were the first to celebrate. The union of the crowns
marked an end to centuries of conflict and the dawn
of a new age for Scotland.

The King assured us that the union would benefit both
countries. That Scotland's identity would be maintained. And
that good times were just around the corner.

But James has not kept his promises.

*First chance he got he was off to the flesh pots of London.
And he hasn't looked back.*

James tells us he can best serve Scotland's
interests from London.

Come off it sir! If you're so keen on Scotland, why don't you
come back and visit occasionally?

Call Me James I

A Controversial New Review of our King

JAMES VI OF SCOTLAND and the first of England had good cause to want be out of Scotland. His upbringing under the control of George Buchanan, one of Mary Queen of Scots friends, had been strict to the point of cruelty.

He had lived in a constant state of penury - at least for a king. Turning against all of Buchanan's philosophies, he had embraced a belief that the law was nothing else but the command of the sovereign. Democracy was not the natural order of things as all men were not equal. He also became very antagonistic to the Presbyterians and became set on Episcopacy, rule by bishops, as the favoured form of worship.

He never really knew his mother Mary Queen of Scots. In principle he felt that he should stand up for her, when she was under house arrest in England. In reality he was far more concerned to inherit the throne of England and unite the two countries. When she died at the hand of the executioner at Elizabeth's orders he took it as a personal insult, but dared not do anything in case it affected his succession. He lost of lot of Scottish support for his inactivity even though the Scots had deposed Mary.

When he went to England he was able to rule Scotland by post through the Scottish Privy Council. 'This I must say for Scotland: here I sit and govern it with my pen, I write and it is done, and by a Clerk of the Council I govern Scotland now, which others could not do by the sword.'

He addressed the problem of constant fighting. Two major acts of dealing with it stand out. He authorised the complete extinction of the MacGregors, who were particularly notorious, a deed well supported by all the neighbours who had suffered over the years. He then hanged his cousin Earl Pate, Patrick Stewart of the Orkneys, a particularly sadistic and violent man.

Once he had moved down to England he returned only once to Scotland and that was to impose the Five Articles of Perth on a reluctant General Assembly and an outraged people.

Name Game Shame of James VI

Rotten Royal James VI is at it again.

<u>Last week he unveiled the new union flag - a loony mixture of the St George's Cross and the St Andrews Cross. The Scots don't like it. The English don't like it. So why do it?</u>

Now he says the names Scotland and England should be dropped altogether. The new name for his kingdom? ***Great Britain.*** That'll never catch on.

We say: enough is enough!

A unified flag will never be popular. A single Parliament just wouldn't work.

It's time the crackpot king ended these daft schemes.

Postcards from the Old Country
by Diana J. Weinstein III

Visited Glamis Castle today. Apparently it's haunted. Really wanted to see the Grey Lady but the vibrations seemed very friendly. They gave us a whisky tasting before the tour of the castle. After that we had lunch in the local pub and we had to try some Tennents Extra. Extra what, I wondered? After sherry trifle and a coffee with whisky I needed the ladies. I couldn't work the light switch, the door wouldn't lock and I fell down the stairs! Could it have been the Grey Lady making a poltergeist attack on me?
Diana

Dundee Area Sewerage and Waste Treatment Works, Angus.

Plague of Green Ladies

Epidemic of Ghosts Gripping Scotland

REPORTS ARE coming in from all over the country of a new menace which threatens many of Scotland's most prominent buildings. One worried laird was come forward.

Lord Murray, 45, from his castle of Huntingtower near Perth, said: 'Things have got beyond a joke. There is enough trouble in these times of warfare and turmoil, without this as well. My Lady Greensleeves has haunted the castle for some time now. She bangs on walls, blows out lights, and opens and closes doors. She is terrifying the servants. Her apparition keeps appearing at windows worrying the chickens. When are the authorities going to something about this? Can't our great reformed church do something?'

Green Ladies, which are ghosts either dressed in green or giving off an eerie green light, are over-running the country. These days virtually every castle, church or other building has its own spectre. There are also Grey Ladies, White Ladies, as well as Pink,

Blue and Black. Other supernatural phenomena include poltergeists, predictor spirits and stress apparitions. All too much for many who have to live in these buildings.

A spokesman for the church said: 'While we do our best to exorcise as many of these ghosts as possible, much of their appearance is castle owner's own fault.

'Perhaps they should think about behaving better. Imprisoning your daughter and starving her to death, or murdering your relatives in the castle dungeon, is just asking for trouble. If you are arguing with your wife, perhaps you should refrain from strangling her. Hanging servants or pedlars for no good reason should also be stopped. Nobody can ever be sure you won't get ghosts but this should at least help.'

Meanwhile, my Lady Greensleeves of Huntingtower refused to comment, although she did issue an icy blast of cold air which froze the balls off the finials above the dormer windows.

King Interferes Once Again

Introduction of the Five Articles of Perth

REMEMBER HIM JAMES VI? He calls himself James I now and lives in England. Well we've already had one James I, and that was enough!

So what's he doing up here then? Interfering as usual. Get a grip on yourself king! You can bully the General Assembly, but we don't want your Five Articles and we don't want your bishops. The first four articles are bad enough, but kneeling to receive communion you must be off your throne! Even if we have to wait 20 years for this rubbish to be rescinded we'll wait. Until then let's boycott them and see what the Courts of the High Commission try to do.

The king says that he wants to standardise religious practice in Scotland and England. So what! Him and his Anglican chums can do what they want. We're going to stick two fingers up to him and stick to the right way: the Scottish way!'

I mean let's face it, James VI has come to Scotland only once since he also became King of England, and that has been to force these Five, so-called, Articles of Perth on what we believe was an extremely reluctant General Assembly. And do you want you know what the Five articles are: that the festivals of the Christian year should be observed, that confirmation should be administered by bishops not ministers, that private communion and private baptism should be allowed in case of serious illness and can you believe it? That communion should be received kneeling!

As these were all things that had been thrown out by our Presbyterians it was unlikely that we were going to welcome them back. It would seem that it wasn't just your correspondent but the general populace who were furious too. A round of applause for the ministers who have refused to have anything to do with it and well done those congregations who boycotted the service. We can proudly say that they have been ignored.

Will it be 20 years before the General Assembly meets again? Even if it takes that long they should still be rescinded.

We have demonstrated again that royal interference in liturgical matters will not be accepted in Scotland and it has hardened public opinion against the sovereign.

Obituary

James VI

Finally his dream came true and James became king of the whole of mainland Britain. However, his policy of exterminating the people then living in Ireland and replacing them with incomers from the mainland will live on and on. James is succeeded by his son, Charles I.

Open Season Declared on MacGregors

KING CHARLES I has issued a letter of Fire and Sword and declared open season on MacGregor hunting. Although they were kept in check by James VI, in recent years they have committed further raids in Menteith, Angus, Clackmannan, the Lennox, the Mearns, Perth and Stirling. The cull means it is now legal to kill MacGregors and hunt them with bloodhounds.

A preservation movement has already rallied to help the MacGregors. A spokesman said yesterday: 'This cull could lead to the MacGregor becoming an endangered species. They may do a lot of damage with their raids and anti-establishment sentiments, but that is no reason to hunt them to extinction. Properly trained, they make ideal pets.'

Several well-known stars of stage and screen are rumoured shortly to joint the campaign.

Prayer Book Sinks At Launch

WE SPOKE TO some of the rioters in St Giles, Edinburgh.

'Not enough jokes.'

'We were expecting something a bit lighter.'

'... and a few pictures wouldn't have gone amiss.'

'I went to the launch party. The food was atrocious and such small portions.'

'I think the king is claiming a hotline to God with it, the bit about Royal prerogative - I don't agree with that!'

'Aye, that's a bad thing.'

'And it's got those bloody Five Articles of Perth again. I thought we'd seen the last of those.'

Key Fact

The Prayer Book came to be seen as a not very good idea by a particularly unsuccessful king. Charles I managed to come up with terrible ideas all his life. This one led to riots, then to the signing of the National Covenant in 1638 and the condemnation of episcopacy by the General Assembly.

It's OK, Jimmy: God's on Our Side!

The National Covenant is Signed in the Presence of the Almighty

THE ANNOUNCEMENT was made today: "It's official now. We have it in writing! It's a legally binding contract between Scotland and God. God hasn't been able to sign yet, as he's gone to Largs today, but the rest of us from Dull to Drem and all towns in between have been adding our marks! So why don't you join in, sign the Covenant and you'll get a nice cup of tea and a plain biscuit."

This is our new Covenant. It's been drawn up by Alexander Henderson, a minister and Archibald Johnson, an advocate. It is the latest of many covenants that we Scots have had with God. This one, the National Covenant, was created directly in response to the introduction by the current king, the so-called Charles I, and his Book of Common Prayer. It may seem strange to outsiders that such a simple thing as a prayer book should cause such ill feeling. But when you read between the lines you can see that Charles was claiming divine right for himself. He was removing the freedom from our church and of our Presbyterian principles. In addition, the services were being anglicised. Is it any wonder we are angry?

As our readers know, we all have responded by renewing the covenant of 1581, which had been prepared by John Knox. It's been revised and expanded to take account of the modern world we all live in. Our National Covenant publicly states that Scotland is in a direct relationship with God. We are free from the interference of both the King and the Catholic Church and 'all kinds of Papistry'!

We Comment

The Covenant demands a free parliament and General Assembly that does not include an Episcopal system, a system where royalty can appoint bishops.

To many of us the Covenant is unreadable. It is couched in long words and legalese. But we say it binds the nation in a contract with God. We Scots are now the chosen ones. We believe up to 300,000 people have signed – freely we say: duress has not been positively proved in any case. This is one in the eye for Charles I and the English.

The Covenant draws a huge number of people together. Some say it alienates everyone else and that conflicts will arise between those wanting to endorse it and those completely against it.

We say that even centuries from now, many Scots will still be unable to discuss it without strong feelings being raised.

Key Fact

The catalyst that sparked off the National Covenant was Charles I. His prayer book, however beautifully written, was seen as part of a Catholic plot to destroy the Presbyterian Church. He was just too far away, too autocratic and too dogmatic.

Lawyers Should Put Own House in Order

HOW LONG MUST Edinburgh citizens suffer the behaviour of the legal profession?

For too long, prominent lawyers and judges have haunted the dives of the city centre at all hours. It is not unusual to find two or three most honourable Lords of Session mounting the bench in the forenoon in a crapulous state. One of our sources, who does not wish to be named, states that he eminent judge Lord Newton, 'considered himself as only better fitted for business that he had just imbibed six bottles of claret...' And even the court itself is not safe. It is well-known that many judges take their bottles of wine into court with them. Something should be done about these legal louts.

City Issues Plague Warning

EDINBURGH CITIZENS are taking risks by ignoring health and safety advice about plagues, the City council warned this week.

Streets affected include all those within the city boundary wall and it is thought that even the countryside will be affected.

Council officials called on Edinburgh residents to travel as little as possible and hit out at those still making unnecessary visits to friends and relatives.

Warning notices have been posted in affected streets and plague-hit households have been identified with painted crosses.

A council official gave the following statement: 'I would appeal to people to act sensibly and respect the notices and the reason why they have had to be put up. We are in the middle of an extremely serious situation and inconsiderate action by individuals could have further serious consequences.'

In addition, there have been calls to clean up Edinburgh's streets. Not for nothing is the town called 'Auld Reekie'. The ten PM call of 'gardy loo' as chamber pots are emptied into the street leads to the waste of ten or eleven floors in each land pouring into the streets. The streets stink and vermin are everywhere. Sedan chairs are increasingly favoured by the wealthy so that they can travel without their shoes having to touch the streets.

A prominent physician said yesterday: 'This is a panic situation. I can assure people that, while streets piled high with human waste are unpleasant, there is absolutely no reason to think that the situation is actually injurious to health. And as for all this nonsense about rats spreading the plague, people are just clutching at straws. We are near a busy port, Leith, and the black rats come off the ships.'

We asked whether it would be possible for rats to carry plague.

'If they've all got it, then why aren't they all dead? There is no medical evidence that rats can carry plague.'

City Plague Street Sealed

EDINBURGH OFFICIALS took radical action to contain the plague this week with the sealing off of Mary King's Close in the city centre. The street, occupied by a cross-section of Edinburgh society, was so badly hit by disease that the decision was taken to seal all exits and hope that the plague would burn itself out.

Shocked onlookers told of the heavy-handed attitude of council officials as they went about their work. High Street resident Violet Venison said 'They didn't let anyone out, they just built these walls at either end of the street. Even when people tried to escape, they just stuffed them back in again and kept on building.' Ms Venison, 46, continued: 'You could hear people screaming for days, trying to

get out. It was a terrible thing to hear. I had to put earplugs in and have a whisky before I could sleep.'

Now local residents are complaining about the smell issuing from the sealed street. A council spokesman said: 'Some people are never happy. We contain the plague as best we can and they quibble over the stench of decaying corpses.' When asked what steps the council would take to resolve this sanitation problem, he admitted that they had not yet found anyone who would go in and remove the corpses but that it was only a matter of time before volunteers came forward who were sufficiently desperate for money.

Then he added: 'But it's not my department anyway.'

Postcards from the Old Country
by Diana J. Weinstein III

Still in Edinburgh, I went on the Ghostly Pub Tour. After drinks in 14 pubs we went on a tour of Mary King's Close. It's like this old street which was walled up with plague victims inside - then they built the City Chambers on top of it to make sure none of them could get out. It's real spooky, you walk down there and you can just imagine this narrow twisty street and when you look up, you almost expect to see the sky. (In fact you just see the City Chambers plumbing.) Anyway I was well wrapped up in my crop top and Manolo Blahniks but I felt an icy chill down there. When the tour guide saw me shivering, he explained that that was where ghosts are sometimes felt! What is it about me that I attract this kind of phenomena? Diana

Gayfield Square Police Station, Edinburgh

Charles I Let Off Lightly

English Execute Our King

WHAT ARE THE ENGLISH playing at? They've gone soft. They should look to us Scots when they want to see how to deal with a difficult monarch. Oh yes we've got through a fair few kings so I think we can safely say we know what we're doing. Crivvens, cutting off someone's head, at the very least they could have sliced his stomach open and showed him what his insides look like.

We didn't like him, and we didn't like his ideas but this paper thinks it was bad mistake to kill him. What the hell, it'll give us all a damn good chance to have another go at the English. This time we're going to give them a good thrashing. We'll bloody Cromwell's nose and stick his warts in the mud!

We spoke to one of the top Covenanting ministers about the plan of campaign and he had this to say to us. 'I can't see any reason why we shouldn't beat the proverbial pants off them. We've had a bit of a chat about this and we're going to advise David Leslie, the Scottish Commander, to attack Cromwell and the evil sinners who make-up his army at Dunbar.'

'Of course the first thing we need to do is gather the troops together. Then we will purge them of all the ungodly elements.'

Rather alarmed, we asked him if that wouldn't mean that all the professional soldiers would be left out? But he had a ready and convincing answer. 'The army will be made up of the devout, the holy the chosen ones of God! You don't think God would let them down? Once we get to the high ground overlooking Dunbar we will advocate a mad charge down, destroying the cursed worshippers of the Devil. We'll throw them into the sea and they will surely receive their punishment, first from us and then God.'

This paper is not completely convinced that these would be the best tactics to get our own back on the English. But we are confident that this prediction is unlikely to happen. If David Leslie's plans to starve them out are stuck to, we think they will bear more fruit.

But let's give Cromwell a hearty Scottish welcome at Dunbar and roast his vitals over a good peat fire.

Breaking News ...

Own Goal

Battle of Dunbar Disaster

Scots Slaughtered

'Well Tommy, a lot of critics would say' etc...

Biggest Congregations Ever, Boast Ministers

Act of Parliament Fines People for Non-Attendance at Church

'We're packing them in,' claimed the stone-faced minister of St Ninian's at Alyth. 'They can't get enough of what the Kirk has to offer! We've even been thinking of starting up a 'stone the unbelievers club', but we had to put it on hold since there aren't any unbelievers around here.' He allowed a slight smile to hover briefly in the general area of his lips.

Key Fact

Charles II went back to the last parliament of 1633 and, with the Act Recissory, all legislation passed since then was declared null and void. It meant that legally Scotland was back to where it had been before the execution of Charles I. Charles tried to re-establish bishops, but this led to wide-spread discontent from Covenanters.

They've All Got It In for Me

Are the Covenanters paranoid?

DOES LIFE SEEM HARD? Have you got your troubles? Meet Protestant fanatic James Mitchell. He claims that everywhere he goes people are trying to kill him because of his religious beliefs.

'All I want is to praise the lord in peace and quiet without the interference of a load of bishops appointed by the king. What do they know about life in Fife? Have they ever scraped a living from rocky fields, or milked goats for a living?'

And you think they're out to get you?

'Think? I only managed to get to this interview, here in Edinburgh, by crawling through the sewers at dead of night. I've been chased through Scotland, by that damnable Archbishop Sharp in his fancy coach. He'll come to a sticky end if he goes through Fife unprotected, I say. He always was a Royalist and he's certainly lining his own pockets now that Charles II is on the throne.'

Aren't you just being just a bit precious? OK you're a Presbyterian but do you really think the Bishops don't like you?

'They hate us because we want don't want them and their sponging off good working folk. We're against everything they stand for. Take that Pope with his grand palaces and flunkies and his edicts from on high. We want nothing to do with him and we want him to have nothing to do with us. As for the bishops and the rest of the Episcopalians they can go and stew in the juices of hell. We want to make our own decisions in our own parishes, ministers and laymen equal together.'

Seems an appealing thought. But do you all want the same thing?

'Pretty much. Although I admit that there are a few things that we disagree over and we've had a few splits. But then if you want religious freedom we have to accept that my religious needs might not be exactly like yours. Anyway I'd best go now. I brought my gun down and I'm going to have a pot-shot at Sharp. Who knows I might get lucky? If I don't there's always Magus Moor!'

Thatcher is Evil Witch

Further Witch Case Strikes Haddington

IT IS FEARED that there may be another witch 'panic', following the prosecution of Mairgret the Thatcher by Haddington Presbytery. Mairgret was accused of various crimes against the general population, acts so vile and vicious that they threatened the very fabric of society. The case is to be passed to the authorities in Edinburgh, but it is expected that Mairgret will be executed in the following weeks. Despite her wickedness, she remains unrepentant.

Her case follows decades of witchcraft prosecutions since James VI made it a hobby following the famous North Berwick trials in 1590. His book *Daemonologie* has rarely been off the best-selling list.

Baillie David Seton of Haddington told us: 'Witchcraft is all around us. There are simply scores of women huddled in their hovels making incantations and sticking pins in dolls; or dancing, gossiping and even smiling. We need to hunt these wicked women down, then garotte and burn them, the scheming harlots. I would estimate that by the 1720s we will have executed thousands of women, and even a few men. It is my duty as a man of God to find and kill everyone who doesn't agree with me, er, the word of God.'

He went on: 'Some people have claimed that torturing and maiming people until they confess is unjust and cruel. I say that to cleanse our society any means are justified. And hey, if we torture and burn some of the wrong people it will encourage others to behave better.'

Since speaking to this paper, Baillie Seton has himself confessed to wizardry, sorcery, demonic pact, necromancy, hydromancy, charming and fornicating with a frog. After he was executed by burning, it came to light that a court official had transposed his name with that of an accused witch. We would like to extend our condolences to his family and the other 12 warlock badgers in his coven.

A Sharp Exit!

ARCHBISHOP JAMES SHARP has been murdered at Magus Moor in Fife. His death marks the culmination in growing discontent with church policy, Sharp himself and King Charles II.

Archbishop James Sharp had become one of the great enemies of the Covenanters. So who was he?

A clever young cleric, James Sharp left Scotland after the National Covenant of 1638. He was a royalist and spent much time in London in prison. Because he was an intelligent man skilled at negotiating, he was freed by Cromwell and sent back to Scotland to represent Scottish Church grievances.

At the restoration of Charles II he was made Archbishop of St Andrews. He became an example of what the Presbyterians hated about the bishops: trying to impose his religious programme on the populace while at the same time lining his own pockets.

In 1668 he was shot at in Edinburgh by a Covenanting extremist who missed, but now he was been brutally murdered at Magus Moor. The Covenanters finally caught up with him.

Key Fact

When the Covenanters killed Archbishop Sharp (they shot, slashed and trampled him, then crushed his skull – all this in front of his daughter) they were actually planning to ambush someone else. They then, however, searched his body for signs of witchcraft. It is quite interesting that many Covenanters demonstrated very little of the Christian attributes of forgiveness and non-violence.

Horoscope

James VII 1633-1701
Watch out for the sins of the flesh, unless you want to risk an ignominious disease in later life.

We've Been Tangoed!

New King is William of Orange!

REJOICE FELLOW SCOTS there's a new king! Bill the husband of Mary, James's VII's daughter. We've got rid of the perfidious Stewart. Yes James VII has gone at last. What was he on? Trying to give the same rights to Catholics as if it was a proper religion, we didn't like it and we're pretty sure that God was against it too.

Now we have a proper king, a Protestant king, with a decent and wholesome way of worshipping God. None of that Popery, with its incantations and incense burning. Such heathen practices are better suited to the Continentals and the French in particular, rather than a civilised country like Scotland. God knows what they get up to. The Catholics probably just tell the witches off rather than burning them!!

It's not all settled yet though. We suspect those smarmy Jacobites will probably start raising armies to try to overthrow the legitimate king. Lay off we say. He was confirmed by the 1689 Scottish Convention. It's all down there in writing and whatever they say, it is not of 'dubious legality', Jimmy.

We must, though, be ever alert! *The Daily Chippie* says watch out for John Graham of Claverhouse, Viscount or 'Bonnie Dundee', as he is known by the more sycophantic papers. 'Bloody Clavers' as we like to call him. Our tipster has 2-1, getting into a big battle at Killiecrankie and 3-2 it'll be in 1689. His prediction is for a Jacobite win. However we think it will probably be an empty victory – the tea-leaves suggest that Dundee could come to a sticky end there. Stick some money on: you're not going to win much but you'll come out ahead.

Breaking News ...

VISCOUNT DUNDEE has won the battle at Killiecrankie against King William's army led by General Hugh Mackay. However Dundee has been mortally wounded, hit by a bullet. He was a brave fighter and tactician, although a dirty Jacobite. Without his skill and personality, the Jacobites have lost heart. The Highlanders have no rallying point and became frustrated besieging Perth and Dunkeld were frustrated. They have retreated and mostly disbanded.

James VII has also returned and showed bravery by landing in Ireland but thankfully was defeated at the Battle of the Boyne in 1690 and then retreated to France. Sadly, he ended his life recognised as brave and honest, even by *The Daily Chippie*, but also as the silliest man the French court had seen.

Key Fact

A fleeing redcoat from Killiecrankie leapt across the River Garrie: a massive jump that left the pursuing Jacobites astounded and unable to follow.

Obituary

James VII

The general feeling is that James VII's reign got worse the longer it went on. It is thought that he contracted syphilis on one of his philandering adventures, which affected his judgement. Or maybe he was just an idiot like so many of his forbears.

Massacre of Glencoe

Morning Edition

Violence Erupts After Fun Night Out

REPORTS HAVE come in of a bit of high spirits at Glencoe. Troops staying in the Glen with friends have been involved in high spirits. Sadly it appears that some of the locals were slightly hurt during the evening. Young men and alcohol, eh? But we've got to give them the chance to let off steam every now and then.

Lunchtime Edition

Some Serious Injuries

THE LATEST news from the Glen is that some of the residents were badly hurt to the point of being dead. Of course while we should always condemn violence on any scale, these things do happen. The initial boisterous behaviour does seem to have escalated. There has been bad blood between the Mac-Donalds of Glencoe and the Campbells. Settling it in this way is typical of the Highlanders and we shouldn't really expect anything more.

Afternoon Edition

Campbells Murder MacDonalds!

THE DELIBERATE KILLING of MacIan his family and 38 members of his clan will appall all civilised citizens. For taking the opportunity to exact revenge for some slight in the distant past, Robert Campbell and his troops should be dealt with swiftly by the authorities. This terrible crime is beyond forgiveness. The murderers were even being billeted with the people they slaughtered.

Evening Edition

Death in the Glen: Government Cover-up?

THE SLAUGHTER of the Mac-Donalds was not clan treachery but the result of a deliberate order. We have identified that this was a military operation authorised by no less a person than King William, through his agents, particularly John Dalrymple, Master of Stair. And this paper would like to be the first to call the nine of diamonds 'the Curse of Scotland' as a reference to his coat of arms, which has nine lozenges on it. Clever, eh?

It was a deliberate political move to put the Jacobites and Episcopalians on the back foot. It would appear that MacIan and his clan were chosen both for their choice of religion and for their general lawlessness.

We say, bad show!

The Massacre

The Place: Glencoe
The Time: Now

This just in. Thirty-eight members of the MacDonald clan have been murdered by a force composed mainly of Campbells. Women and children were not spared. And the massacre hinged on an act of gross betrayal.

We Name the Guilty Parties

The Campbells - once a proud clan, heroes of the age of Wallace and Bruce - have long been the eyes and ears of the English. And with their continual feuds with the MacDonalds, among others, they were more than willing to lift their swords against their rival clan.

But This is No Clan Feud

This slaughter was initiated by the King, William of Orange himself, through his man, John Dalrymple, Master of Stair. Dalrymple has recently been in the news, as the man in charge of the Royal Ordinance that all Highland Chiefs of Highland clans must abandon the old Stewart loyalty and swear fealty to William of Orange.

Let us not forget that a large portion of Scots Highlanders are still Catholic, due mostly to the 'Auld Alliance' with France. Many of them had been in rebellion over the exile of King James VII and II - the 'Jacobite' rebellions against William and Mary. And they were being asked to swear loyalty to the anti-Catholic, anti-Stewart, anti-Highlander King - from Holland!

The closing date for the Oath was New Years Day, 1692.

One chieftain, MacIan of Clan MacDonald, tried to take his oath at Fort William only to be told that the proper place was Inveraray. He arrived there two days late due to this misdirection and the bitterly cold weather. The sheriff who was to receive his oath was even later, but on arrival, accepted MacIan's oath.

The Plot Unfolds

However, Dalrymple viewed the oath invalid because it was two days late and ordered the Campbells to do a 'job' for him. The leader was to be Robert Campbell of Glenlyon. His task was to exterminate the detested MacDonalds.

We Print The Actual Orders For The Slaughter

To Captain Robert Campbell of

# of Glencoe

Glenlyon 'For Their Majesties' Service'

Sir, You are hereby ordered to fall upon the rebels, the M'Donalds, of Glencoe and putt all to the sword under seventy. You are to have special care that the old fox and his sons doe upon no account escape your hands. You are to secure all the avenues, that no man may escape. This you are to putt in execution at five o'clock in the morning precisely, and by that time, or very shortly after it, I'll strive to be att you with a stronger party. If I doe not come to you att five, you are not to tarry for me, but to fall on. This is by the King's special command, for the good of the country, that these miscreants be cutt off root and branch. See that this be putt in execution without feud or favour, else you may expect to be treated as not true to the king's government, nor a man fitt to carry a commission in the king's service. Expecting you will not faill in the fulfilling hereof as you love yourself, I subscribe these with my hand. Master of the Stair (John Dalrymple)

The 'old fox' was the clan Chief of the MacDonalds. The king was William of Orange.

The Betrayal - A First-Hand Report

Survivors' eyewitness accounts say that the Campbells, led by Sir Robert Campbell, claimed they were lost in the snow. The MacDonalds welcomed the Campbell men and their Highland allies into their humble dwellings, fed them meat and ale, and offered their friendship. Reportedly, romance even blossomed among the younger folk.

Suddenly, without warning, the Campbells stirred into action at five o'clock in the morning. They set about slaughtering all the defenceless and unsuspecting MacDonalds they could find.

Wife's Gold Ring Horror

After killing the MacDonald Chief, the murderers abused his wife, and a soldier bit the finger off her hand to get her gold ring. She was left to die in the cold along with many of the clan who escaped but perished from exposure. Estimates put the number of those slain at as many as 38, including Ian, the Chief, and his family.

Down the Pan!

Commercial Failure at Darien

£400,000 raised and what have we got to show for it now? Very little indeed – given that the money and the stock have gone, not to mention that a goodly proportion of our citizens who went out to Darien are dead. It can't be seen as a total success!

So whose fault was it? The English! In particular we say the buck stops at the door of the East India Company. They were one of the real villains that caused this failure. It was them and the House of Lords that stopped us from making a real go of this venture. Withdrawing capital at the worst moment, refusing to trade with our representatives out in Panama, and spoiling our chances with those who settled in America. Not very gentlemanly behaviour!

There has been uninformed talk that it wasn't the best site for a new trading post. People have said that it was swampy. Some of the settlers complained of the new varieties of flies, bugs and blood-sucking insects in Darien. Pah, we've got midges here in Scotland. There was some nonsense that it wasn't a very healthy place. That it was riddled with fever – crivvens, there are plenty of towns in Scotland that are disease ridden and we don't complain about them. So, the Spanish thought it was theirs. Well tough Johnny Spaniard. But let's face it when it comes down to the bit, it was all the fault of the English.

We talked to William Patterson who was the chief executive. *What's it all about?*

'It was a Company of Scotland trading to Africa and the Indies. We set it up to take advantage of foreign trading. It should have worked. We were going to raise half the money in England. But when we were trying to do this, I think we upset some of the other commercial interests. Well I suppose they were fighting their own corners and wanted to protect their investments. But it was the English East India Company in particular who managed to stymie the raising of capital in England and worse, abroad.'

What made you think you could pull this off?

'Well I was a founder of the bank of England, I have plenty of enthusiasm, but I suppose I may have got a bit too passionate about the whole thing. When I couldn't raise the money in England, I set up shop in Scotland and we raised the money there: £400,000.'

A bit of a tidy sum, wasn't it? In fact, half the amount of capital available in Scotland at the time. The expression eggs and basket does present itself.

'Thank you for sharing your thoughts. Anyway, the first ships set off with high hopes in 1698. But once they got to Darien and started to set up shop apparently it didn't seem such a good idea. Contrary to our expectations there was no one to sell to, no one to buy from, disease was rampant, and we had lots of trouble with the Spanish. But before news could get back the second expedition had set off. Things weren't really improving and they in their turn were unable to stop the third expedition.

'Oh, we struggled on for a few years but the end of the company came about with the Union between England and Scotland. But I would like to say that the miscarriage of our plans did contribute to the Union! The need in Scotland for both cash and for trade outlets forced the issue. You know one of the key elements of the Union was a cash reparation to Scotland to cover the money lost in the Darien Venture?'

We say: BLAME IT ON THE ENGLISH

COMMENT

Act of Security is Scotland's Insurance

<u>England is at it again.</u>

Not content with their ideas to unite the Parliaments of Scotland and England, the spin doctors have come up with another one. Force a new monarch on us. A foreigner.
If Queen Anne leaves no heir, the English have decided the successor should come from the House of Hanover. And as usual, there's been no consultation with Scotland. Yet again they expect us to go along with their high-handed schemes.

But WE won't stand for it!

<u>For too long we have tholed the English and their interference in our ways. The Rough Wooing in 1544. The new Prayer Book in 1637. Cromwell's invasion of the 1650s. The Killing Times of 1689. The list goes on.</u>

Well it stops here!

The Act of Security is Scotland's guarantee of a say in the succession. It opts for a potentially different choice on the death of Anne.

And take note. The Act orders preparations for hostilities.
Preparations which every true Scot should make.
We'll show the English that Union's not for us.

The Union

What It Means for You!

It's a disgrace! As a result of this sell out, in 300 years from now there will hardly be a native Scots speaker in our country. We'll all be speaking – and your reporter can hardly bear to write the word: *English*. We shudder at the thought.

Save our language now!

Union Signed, Duty Raised!

THE TREATY OF UNION has now been sorted out and the great and the good just need to rubberstamp it, 'dot the Ts and cross the Is'. Your correspondent understands that it should be done and dusted by April or May 1707.

But, the question we all want to know is, will it be good for the ordinary Scotsman in the street?

We spoke to Archibald Campbell, 3rd Duke of Argyll, or Islay as his friends know him.

'So, can I call you Archie?'

'Only if you'd like to spend the rest of your life in a bottle dungeon.'

'Ha, ha, your Grace. I am of course ever your servant. So this Union, what's in it for us?'

'As you know in 1707 Scotland is currently a very poor country with low prospects, little trade except with England, and most institutions dominated by the Kirk. The English putting the screws on us with the Alien Act in 1705 didn't improve things.'

'The Alien act, sounds spooky, what was that?'

'It was a law which would stop Scots owning land in or trading with England.'

'That doesn't sound fair?'

'No, but to give them a little credit, it was a device to force us to the negotiating table. The Scots and the English had been like a married couple – always scrapping, but deep down knowing that we'd be stronger united.'

'And this Union?'

'The way the Union has been negotiated will provide Scotland with stability and allow for economic growth, which is good for all of us. It will give us access to the largest free-trade area in the world. We will have a voice in their parliament and we will be sending enough Scots down to the big smoke to adequately represent us. But I have to admit we will have to contribute to the National Debt.'

'You've got to be kidding, your Grace. I think I speak for everyone in Scotland in saying, stuff that. The English ran up the debt so they should pay it!'

'Ah, well normally I'd agree, but there is the hidden debt of some quarter of a million pounds sterling that Scotland still has to pay for our government officers and soldiers in the army.'

'Oh, they spotted that then?'

'I'm afraid so. And we're still out of pocket from the Darien adventure. We've agreed something called the "Equivalents". In short Scotland will be getting £400,000.'

'Wow! What else?'

'Well obviously there'll have to be standardisation so that our systems work together.'

'And by that, your Grace, you mean tax!'

'In one word, that may or may not be one of the areas that as a group of parliamentarians, together with our colleagues and after much consultation may possibly consider.'

'I hope you're not putting it on the salt. Or heaven forbid, the malt!'

'We are also pleased to announce that by 1740 Glasgow should be a major centre for the tobacco trade in Western Europe.'

'So you're going to tax both salt and malt! By the Almighty.'

'Well I must be off. I have enjoyed this interview and look forward to the next one.'

They Think It's Hanover: It Is Now ...

At last a king!

Seven years with a woman on the throne was seven years too many. This paper is very pleased to announce that the new king will be George I. It's about time we had a man on the throne.

We know some people will carp: 'He doesn't speak English', 'He spends most of his time in Hanover!'

But let's face it, he's not a Catholic and do we really want any more Jameses. We've had seven, isn't that enough? Let's try a new name on the throne. Anyway what could go wrong? Parliament is much stronger now.

Well, he might put his wife in prison and there may be constant bickering with his son and there could be a crisis with the South Sea Company but in the end it will lead to greater prosperity.

And who knows when his son, George II, does take over by the 1750s Britain should be doing great, we'll probably have an empire and the Stewarts – who to be honest have not been a great success – will be history.

Don't Spoil My Petunias

Jacobite Rising: Earl of Mar Leads the Rebels

AT THE START of all this, the Earl of Mar was slighted in London! 'He's just a big girl's blouse', said a prominent member of the Whig party. 'I'm not,' said Mar, when he reached Fife and had raised an army.

Well, we say it's quite right that the Duke of Argyll should be sent up to do something. Yes maybe it is unfair that he is a professional soldier, but Mar has got to learn his lesson. An expert comments: 'Mar hasn't demonstrated much understanding of war up to this point, but will he now?'

The first reports said that initially Mar got down to some good solid marching about, sword rattling and letting off muskets, but we understand that his 12,000 troops then got stuck at Stirling. They were apparently held up by Argyll's army of 4,000 troops. Our man in Leith then forwarded information that some of Mar's troops under Brigadier Mackintosh got to the town; they were joining up with some English supporters to make a combined force. They then seem to have gone down to Preston but the secondary reports show that they were soon forced to surrender.

As the reports came in thick and fast, we established that there was a battle at Sheriffmuir, near Dunblane. Mr 'girl's blouse' despite outnumbering the Duke of Argyll's troops was forced to admit defeat.

And what about the other cast members? Well we learn that the Old Pretender, James VIII, has been hanging around in Scotland for a while. In typical fashion he managed to avoid reaching the battlefield until after the fighting had finished – well done Jimmy,

living up to your reputation! So what did he do next? Burnt down a couple of villages in the Ochils. True to form, he felt a bit guilty about that because we learn that he then left some money and headed off back to France.

So what was the Earl of Mar most worried about? The battle, the political developments, the cause? Well, we have an exclusive that during all this armed conflict and rebellious activity, Mar still had time to write to Argyll asking if the Government troops could avoid his garden in Alloa as he'd put a lot of work into it.

We say stick to growing petunias Mar!

SO WE CAN REPORT that the rebellion was quashed but disappointingly the retribution was mild. A number of families have been threatened with losing their lands but in practice it would appear to be only a token gesture. At least they chopped off the head of Viscount Kenmure. He may not have approved, but we say that the best thing to do at the end of an armed rebellion is execute lots of people.

Otherwise, why have we got all these executioners and gallows?

Key Fact

Of the open rebellions in Scotland the 1715 wasn't very exciting. But not the dullest, as there were a couple of Jacobite uprisings that really didn't get off the ground. One where the ships hilariously never landed (1708) and another that left 300 Spanish soldiers stranded (1719). But it was a bit dull!

A Big Yin

Scots Form an Organised Group in Westminster Parliament

IT'S BEEN REVEALED that the Scottish parliamentarian group in Westminster have demanded a 'tall Lord Advocate'. When asked why, they explained, 'we need to see which door he goes through when he votes. Then we can all follow'. It is another example of how we in Scotland lead the world when it comes to democracy!

It's good for Scotland and good for the whole parliament. We should all support our boys in their attempt to engender greater political stability. If we in Scotland benefit, well, that's a side-effect and obviously a good thing. Some moaning minnies have complained that the smaller parties are not getting a look in. Well, we say tough, just grow up and smell the coffee!

Death of Rob Roy MacGregor

All of Scotland has been brought together in grief at the death of Rob Roy. A tragic end. His sobbing wife could barely contain her grief. 'He was only 74!'

We grieve with her for a man synonymous with thieving and blackmail. At Balquhidder local cattle dealers knew to count their fingers after they'd shaken on a deal with him.

Retirement of Witch Burner

IT'S A BLACK DAY: all of Scotland is in mourning. Our witch burner has announced that he is going to retire. 'I've had a good run, but it's time to hang up the old fire-lighting kit and bag of kindling. I shall miss the applause of the crowd, the smoke in my eyes, the garrotting, and the smell of burning flesh. But all good things come to an end.'

But there is some good news for us.

'Come along to Dornoch. I'm going to have a farewell show. There'll be jugglers, pie sellers, pickpockets, ribbon merchants, traders in feathered caps, linen stalls: all the fun of the fair. And, of course, to top the bill I'll be setting fire to a particularly wicked witch.'

We wish him well but Scotland's going to be a duller place without his cheery grin and handy touch with the flint.

Key Fact

Rob Roy stands as a symbol for a number of other figures in Scottish history who are forgotten, but we can't remember who. Elements of his life were turned into a novel by Walter Scott, published in 1817. Like many of his contemporaries, he was driven partly by a sense of loyalty to the Jacobite cause but mainly he had an eye to the main chance in a time of poverty. His great age would have been highly unusual for the eighteenth century.

Comment

ETHNIC CLEANSING - THE WAY FORWARD

There has long been enmity between the Lowlands and the Highlands. While the Lowlands have been influenced by Saxon, Angle and Norman bloodline and culture seeping in from England, the Highlander is descended from the ancient Gael. We know these barbarians as 'wild Irish'. They refuse to speak English, preferring their native Irish tongue of Gaelic. They retain their manner of traditional clothing. They have strange tribal customs and structures. They live in the wilds, not in towns or cities as we do in the Lowlands.

<u>The Highlanders think that their descent from Celtic and Norse stock makes them superior. They see the Lowland Scot as a foreigner and consider us more English than Scottish.</u>

The influence of Malcolm Canmore and his Queen, Margaret, heavily anglicised the Lowlands in the 11th-12th centuries and English became the primary tongue of Edinburgh and other major cities. Indeed, Margaret required interpreters at court meetings as she could speak no Gaelic. But still the Highlanders stick to their Gaelic. Even the translation of the Bible into English leaves them unmoved.

Something must be done about these throwbacks.

The Lowlander and the Highlander are two different races. The Highland barbarians must go. The Highland forests themselves must be swept away for the grand new plan of sheep farming.

<u>And if that means ethnic cleansing, so be it.</u>

Hard times require hard decisions.

'Scots Invented Ethnic Cleansing' Claim

ETHNIC CLEANSING is Scottish in origin and Scottish history may hold the key to solving the current conflicts in the Balkans and elsewhere.

That's the claim of controversial academic Dr Ceilidh Minogue, who says that the influences of various races throughout Scotland's history led to internecine conflict and various attempts at genocide.

'You only have to look at the situation in present-day Bosnia to see clear parallels with Scottish history,' said Dr Minogue from a phone box yesterday. 'Scotland had been occupied by various races, including the Gaels, the Celts, the Picts, the Scandinavians, and the Romans. They all brought their own cultures and ruled their own regions. Then the Normans started making incursions from England and anglicising southern Scotland.

'The Lowland Scots suddenly began to see themselves as a master race, and oppressed the Highlanders. Look at the Clearances, when the Highlanders were forced out of their homes and made to leave the very country to seek new lives abroad - almost like refugees.'

Fumbling for small change, Dr Minogue continued: 'It's just like the situation with the Bosnian Muslims and the Muslian Bosnims, the Sarajevoans and their fight with the ... what is it? Serbs? Serbians? Mesopotininians?'

Then the pips went, and she had to hang up.

We contacted an Edinburgh University academic who confirmed that Dr Minogue's theory may hold some water. 'I know *of* Ms Minogue of course but for once she's come up with quite a good point,' he told us from his desk at the bar in Potterrow Student's Union. 'She's all over the shop with the Bosnian conflict though.'

When pressed for more detail on how ethnic cleansing in Scottish history could be used to resolve the Balkan troubles, our expert told us 'I can't help you I'm afraid, I'm a geologist. I just come in here for the subsidised drink.'

Stewarts Try Again: Second Time Lucky?

YES IT'S THAT TIME AGAIN. But it was the Young Pretender who decided to have a go for the crown. In 1715 Dad had a pop, but had to crawl back across the channel with his tail between his legs. Did the young Charles Edward have what it takes to win the title of king?

His form looked good coming into this one. He'd won high praise at the siege of Gaeta, the teenage prince serving with great courage. But taking on the English on their home ground was always going to be tricky. He needed an away goal to get the campaign off to a good start. But would the young Pretender remain just that - the pretender to the thrones of England and Scotland? And did the Scots really want the Jacobites back?

Landing at Moidart with seven companions, the Seven Men of Moidart,

the force moved to Glenfinnan where the Prince raised his standard. A good showy start. Unfortunately he was already quarrelling with his generals. The high regard he held himself in was starting to be apparent. There was early success at Prestonpans where they had an overwhelming victory over the English forces - albeit a weak force. But there was too much hanging around and then the foolish decision to invade England. A disappointing number of Englishmen, 300, joined the march on London and they finally turned back in November. Would it have made any difference if they had marched on to London?

As it was, they were chased back to Scotland and after one more victory at Falkirk, there is now to be a battle at Culloden, near Inverness.

Scots Butchered by Cumberland Sausage

It's a bloody disaster. What a bunch of useless idiots deciding to fight a pitched battle on open land. My Gran could have done better. And what were they doing crammed into that narrow front between the dykes? Good grief, the Hanoverians must have thought all their Christmases had come at once.

'Oh look, they're all jammed together over there. Shall we shoot in

that general direction on the off chance that we're bound to hit someone or should we go and pick wild flowers until they've sorted themselves out? Oh what the hell, let's just fire our guns!'

This paper says the bonnie Prince is a proper Charlie. And let's hope this was the last pitched battle on British soil.

Unsuccessful Outcome in Young Pretenders Campaign

THE BATTLE OF CULLODEN was a complete disaster for Charles Edward Stewart and since so many of his followers didn't survive, wasn't so good for them either.

Forced marches, lack of food and clothing together with abysmal tactics resulted in as comprehensive defeat as ever a Scots army had suffered. After the battle the Duke of Cumberland certainly earned his nickname as 'The Butcher'. His hatred of Jacobites ensured that revenge was far bloodier than was necessary.

But Prince Charlie rallied his spirits and started to put the blame on everyone else. He then made good his escape. The next five months were spent hiding out in the Highlands, avoiding government troops and moaning that he was being slighted. Throughout this time he remained totally unaware of the appalling poverty of the people trying to help him and the risks they ran. Romantic myths built up around him concentrating on this episode, which were totally undeserved. The true heroes were the likes of Flora MacDonald and the loyal Highlanders, who despite the prince's misgivings and the promise of a reward of the fantastic sum of £30,000, did not betray him.

We predict that the rest of his life will be a slow decline into debauchery and spousal abuse until he finally dies in Rome, the handsome features of his youth long gone, his brave intentions scattered on the field of Culloden.

SENGA'S DIARY
Gender Bending Prince is the Bonniest of All

In his public life, Charles Edward Stewart is a stout-hearted fighting man, the leader and focus of the Jacobite cause. Yet when he sheathes his sword and puts down his buckle, it's time to relax. Then he becomes Betty Burke, a sweet Irish girl. Dressed in a blue and white frock he and his best friend Flora MacDonald often sail across to Skye for a girls' night out at one of the many taverns and night haunts. Girlish giggles can be heard echoing around the island.

From Charles E. Stewart, Prince
Sir

Following the recent article in your 'Senga's Diary' page, I wish to refute the implication that I regularly dress up as a woman. Circumstances were such that I was prevailed upon by my advisers to don a disguise in order to leave the Outer Hebrides. This one occasion can hardly be seen as a habitual activity. I demand that you print an apology and retract this scurrilous article.

Yours in great wrath
Charles Edward Stewart, Prince and younger of the Pretenders.

P. S. I should be king, not that sausage eating Kraut. It's not fair.

Unfit? Try Golf!

COME AND GIVE IT A GO, you may find you like it. It's the new game to delight all your senses. Here's an eager novice. Hi Hamish!

'My first question is where do I start?'

Well, just come on up to St Andrews. Here on the East Coast there is fresh air and plenty of strong cooling breezes. Stay in one of the many friendly guest houses. Remember to bring your own sheets and blankets... and curtains and carpet and knife and fork. And possibly your own bed too.

'You paint a delightful picture. I'm tempted. So, how do I play?'

The game is simplicity itself. You place your ball on the ground and then you try to hit it into a little hole 300 yards away. If you don't get it in first time - and you may not - then you just keep on clubbing away until you do. Keep a note of how many hits it takes you to get it into the hole. The one with the lowest number wins.

'It sounds fascinating. Is that all there is to it?'

Well we have a very long rule book and we're thinking of introducing a dress code: brightly patterned sweaters and trousers that are too short. We're thinking of calling it sports casual and we hope it might just catch on with the fashion pack. Sound like your kind of game?

'It sure does. An excellent way to waste an afternoon and I imagine plenty of time for drinking in the evening.'

Well, Hamish is going to take it up. What about you? We have one free round to give away, the hire of clubs is only 10 shillings a round. Send a postcard to our Scottish History editor explaining why you haven't got anything better to do for five hours during the middle of the day and enter now.

Letters to the Editor

From Minister Alexander Stoniface
Sir
Both my parishioners and myself were appalled by what we heard of the so-called Prince Charlie (see previous page). Never have we heard of such brazenness, such an affront to God and such a parleying with the Devil. Poor Mrs Shorthorn went into a terrible decline and has had to read the Bible aloud for the last four days. I myself have been living on grass and praying constantly, in case even reading about it poisoned my immortal soul. We understand he is a Catholic. After writing this letter I shall burn my pen and bury the ashes in unconsecrated earth.
God's Servant,
Alexander Stoniface
P. S. There will be a sale of work at the manse on Saturday morning.

Eligible Enlighteners

THEY'RE THE ARCHITECTS of Scotland's greatest intellectual flowering and at the forefront of modern thinking in philosophy, literature, art and economics. But these boys have got looks as well as brains. So girls, if you're looking for that special man, take a moment to read about Scotland's most eligible.

* **David Hume** - this eminent polymath counts among his hobbies philosophy, law and economy. He is the author of *A Treatise on Human Nature* (1739 and 1740) and a well-known man about town - he is the darling of the coffee-house set. Mind your Ps and Qs though - he is known to despise 'Scotticisms'.

* **Adam Smith** is the author of *Inquiry into the Nature and Causes of the Wealth of Nations* (1776) and his landmark treatise on political economy looks set to be a model for economists for centuries to come. That keen financial mind will come in handy when you're doing the shopping and can't figure out your change.

* **Henry Raeburn** is one of the foremost painters of the age and a keen follower of that principal concern of the Enlightenment, the study of human nature. The ideal date if you fancy getting your parlour redecorated.

Letter of the Week

Edinburgh New Town

2nd March 1770

Sir

What is all this nonsense about building a new town, outside the city walls? Have the city fathers gone mad? I think I speak for all our citizens that we are happy living in Edinburgh as it is. Yes we may have some problems, but sewage in the street is a small price to pay for the opportunity to live so close to your friends and neighbours. This foolish New Town will be socially divisive. Today Earls and lawyers, merchants and ministers, shopkeepers and street sweepers all live in the same building. Guess who'll be moving to this new town? Yes it'll be the rich, leaving the rest of us in the crap.

So to speak.

Your obedient servant,

Tam Brunt Esq

Key Fact

Travel times slashed by 1760. Journeys from Edinburgh to Glasgow reduced from two days to a day and a half.

*James Craig claims ambitious New Town
plans could be in place by 1820 ...*

BOLD NEW ARCHITECTURAL VISION FOR EDINBURGH

A radical plan to transform north Edinburgh into a gracious Grecian-style city was revealed this week, with the city centre management body urging a complete ban on horses, drunkards and open sewers in the streets.

JAMES CRAIG'S competition-winning plan for Edinburgh's new development features monumental buildings, gracious wide streets, and a rational geometric layout. He beat a number of other designers, including an earlier design featuring streets laid out in the shape of a Union Flag. The new buildings are planned to stretch from St Andrew's Square in the East to St George's Square in the West. Street names for the new development honour the Royal Family and include Queen Street, George Street, Hanover Street, Frederick Street and Prince's Street.

The design is set to spark controversy in its sweeping away of traditional medieval designs and its expansion beyond the limits of the city's defensive wall. The wall has been largely abandoned since Flodden but there is a feeling that the city should spread no further into the country. Outraged members of the landed classes slammed the plans, claiming that new buildings creeping into the area between the city centre and the prosperous suburbs would encourage disease and crime.

The plan is a response to the overcrowding in the city centre and an attempt to bring the landed classes back into the city, by creating a completely new suburb for the rich, to be known as Edinburgh New Town. The idea is not a new one and had been proposed by James VII in 1688, but this new design is the most complete visualisation of the concept to date.

Contributing architects, the brothers Robert and John Adam, plan to draw on their travels on the Continent - the 'Grand Tour' - and their controversial work in London to produce the new designs. Much of the style is inspired by classical architecture and some commentators are already describing it as 'the Modern Athens'. In addition Robert Adam has proposed the use of 'bridge streets', with his innovative concept of multi-level town planning, inspired by the Utopian ideas of Leonardo da Vinci.

A council spokesman yesterday described the New Town plans as 'interesting' but said they would probably prove too expensive to realise.

Book Review

Encyclopaedia Britannica (1771)

Amaze Your Friends

Are you often stumped? Want to know how the Spinning Jenny works, what a spruce tree looks like, or how to make a barrel? Ever wondered where Dundee is, who came first, Robert II or Alexander III, or what is a feathery? Then this book is for you! Published in easy-to-read instalments, the *Encyclopaedia Britannica* is a pleasure to own. Find all the answers right now! Comprehensive, authoritative and reasonably priced!

We talked to the editor Mr Smellie, but he was very huffy and insisted his name was pronounced Smiley before he would talk to us. He then threw our reporter out for pretending to hold his nose.

Key Fact

Encyclopaedia Britannica was just one of many such compendia published around the time. It even gave itself a suitably important title page, claiming to be a new work by "the Society of Gentlemen". However it has come to be a major source of information, growing with each subsequent edition. The 1851-1860 edition appears to be the last to be published from Scotland. It now appears in the rather outré CD format.

Raunchy Robbie in Bawdy Ballad Row

ROBERT BURNS is in hot water again with his latest sizzling song.

The shameless star is known for his flamboyance. One of his trademark gimmicks is to scratch his poems on windowpanes using his diamond ring.

And the ploughman poet has just written a controversial song called *Come Rede Me Dame*. Its raunchy lyrics include references to

* **The act of love** ('What length o' graith, when weel ca'd hame/Will sair a women duly')
* **Lust** ('The carlin clew her wanton tail/Her wanton tail sae ready')
* **Size** ('I learn'd a song in Annandale/Nine inch will please a lady')

As a family newspaper we are appalled by this filth. You can find the full text of the song on page two.

Robbie is no stranger to controversy. He is thought to have fathered a string of children by different partners - at the last count he had 14, only five of them born within wedlock. In 1784 he was called to his local kirk to sit on the 'creepie stool' as a public show of shame for fathering another illegitimate child - in this case that of Lizzie Paton. Despite the minister's public tirade remonstrating with him for the sin of houghmagandie, Burns showed no sign of repentance.

We ask: how long can these ploughman poets be allowed to get away with their hell-raising ways?

Robbiemania Hits Edinburgh

THERE WERE SCENES of mass hysteria in Edinburgh yesterday as Robbie Burns, the nation's Number One poet, arrived in the capital. Hordes of poetry fans thronged the streets hoping to catch a glimpse of the star as he rode into town.

The darling of the drawing-room set, Robbie cultivates the image of the rough ploughman. His cheeky chappie persona is enhanced by his reputation as a ladies' man. Lock up your daughters! And your sisters. And your wives.

The poet who made ploughing trendy again has a string of engagements in Edinburgh and gift shops are reporting brisk trade in Robbie memorabilia. Top-selling items are books of poetry, raunchy engravings of the lad himself, and tea-towels.

Lost Burns Poems Rediscovered

CONTROVERSIAL HISTORIAN, Dr Ceilidh Minogue has claimed that she has rediscovered several fragments of Robert Burns poetry. Dr Minogue was in the Globe Inn in Dumfries when approached by a stranger, who gave her the verses in return for two double Balvenie malt whiskies.

An expert in Burns poetry told us: 'Dr Minogue? Don't waste any more of my time!', and hung up. Dr Minogue was not available for comment today, although a cleaner who picked up her phone said she believed Dr Minogue was 'a bit glaikit'. The verses, on the back of beer mats, are as follows:

Holy Willie's Prayer
Weeping Willie sighs sae sair,
Thinking o' his love's lang hair,
But after drinkin' pints o' whisky,
Droopy Willie's nae sae frisky.

The Lords Day
O my Jean says:
There's nae blustering,
O' the summer Sabbath.
Nae dance,
Nae muckle pies,
Nae mountain river song,
Nae o' the Deil's warks,
But Saturday we'll all get canned,
And take loads of drugs.

The Rustic Scotia (Burns Supper)
There's a weel-kent chippie in
   Dundee,
The Rustic Scotia is its name,
It maun hae fair glorious
   suppers,
Which couthie neighbours tak
   awa' hame,
There's haggis, pies and puddins
   white,
A reekin' sicht sae braw
And gar ye want an onion wi' it
Ye can hae an onion ane an a'.

Love Rat Robbie Marries at Last

ROBERT BURNS, the 'ploughman poet', has finally tied the knot.

Long-time lover Jean Armour, pregnant with twins by randy Robbie, has hooked him at last, after being thrown out of her home by her family due to their dalliances together.

Cheeky chappie Robbie told a friend: 'I have taken her to my arms; I have given her a mahogany bed; I have given her a guinea; and I have f**ked her till she rejoiced with joy unspeakable and full of glory...'

Robbiemania has hit the capital with full force over the last two years. With his boyish good looks and trademark ponytail, Burns has graced high society's drawing rooms as a bit of celebrity rough. And the financial rewards have been great. His collection of Scottish Poems, published by John Wilson of Kilmarnock in July 1786, sold 600 copies and was an overnight success, making him the staggering sum of £50. His second volume, published in Edinburgh in April 1787 by William Creech, sold 3000 copies, and is rumoured to have earned him around £800.

Robbie's success has made him an eligible bachelor with a string of affairs.

But one stands out: the enigmatic Clarinda - now revealed as Agnes McLehose, wife of a law agent, mother of four children and a member of respectable Edinburgh society. Despite conducting an exchange of passionate letters between 'Clarinda' and 'Sylvander', Robbie continued to plough his furrow elsewhere. Our sources exclusively reveal that cheating Robbie did not inform his 'Clarinda' of his engagement, leaving her to find out secondhand from his friend Robert Ainslie.

It's thought that a bidding war has already started for coverage of the wedding between rival publications *Hulloo!* and *A'right?*.

Horse Loses Tail in Diabolic Bridge Ordeal

POLICE ARE investigating accusations of witches frequenting a local church. Local man, Mr O'Shanter, claims that he was riding home after a night out at a local tavern. There were lights and music coming from the ruined church at Alloway. O'Shanter, no doubt fortified by drink, investigated. Unfortunately, he called out at one particularly comely witch. There is some confusion as to what happened next, but O'Shanter managed to mount his horse, Meg, and rode for dear life. The witches pursued him, and he only just escaped by riding over the Old Brig o' Doon (witches cannot cross running water). In the melee his mount, Meg, lost her tail. Kate, Mr O'Shanter's wife, told us: 'the man's a blethering blustering drunken blellum'.

Breaking News ...

Following the reports of diabolic happenings at a local church, police have now arrested a man, believed to Mr O'Shanter, and are holding him on animal cruelty charges. Meg, his horse, has been taken into care and may need counselling.

Letter of the Week

Sir

What are all these crofters whingeing about? 'Please sir, we're being dispossessed, please sir we haven't got anything to eat'. Well I say wait for the bicycle to be invented and then get on one and go and look for work. That is the trouble with people today, no gumption!

Thomas T. Brunt Esq

Key Fact

Price of kelp reached £22.00 per ton around about now.

Job Opportunities

Find a new career in sunny Canada. Realise your true potential abroad.

Now, get out of the Highlands before I set fire to your house.

Patrick Sellar

We Don't Want to Miss You but We Think You Ought to Go

The Clearances

TODAY WE'RE LOOKING at the changes in emphasis in agriculture in Scotland over the last few years.

The key element was the redeployment of manpower away from their homes and the introduction of sheep.

We have interviewed both sides in this tricky Clearance issue, first we have a representative from the evil, profit-grabbing, capitalist landlords. 'So, you bunch of bastards, what's your excuse then, Lord MacDonald?'

'Er, well. We can understand your anger. On the face of it, the heartless eviction of people who for generations have lived there does seem a little uncaring. But it was for their own good. The land was becoming overpopulated and it wasn't producing enough food for people to live on. Something had to break. If there wasn't some change then the alternative was starvation and famine.'

'Now Donald, you're a ten-ant. What do you have to say?'

'That's not the whole story. They are forcing us off the land for their profit. We tenants had a bond with our land. Our forefathers and their forefathers and, well, you know, their forefathers had tended to the soil and grown crops and looked after their animals and everything. But no, because the landlords needed a new cravat or the latest bestseller from Walter Scott they just pushed us off the land. Sometimes to the coast and sometimes just to the infertile areas.

'You know what really gets my goat is that often they didn't want us to emigrate because if we did, then they wouldn't have enough soldiers for their armies or workers for the kelp industry.'

Well, there you have it. Brutal removal or an ecological concern for the land?

Next week, a hard-hitting exposé of the tea-room industry: should the tea or the milk go in first?

SCANDAL OF 'GOOD CONDITIONS' AT NEW LANARK

Crackpot Notions of Robert Owen Exposed

New Lanark cotton mills are run along humane lines and the workers are the happiest in Scotland, claims a damning report published in this paper today.

The New Lanark mills - situated in a deep gorge next to the River Clyde - are the largest producers of cotton in Britain. But far from being a traditional Scottish tyrant, the industrialist owner Robert Owen has been revealed as an idealist who puts people before profit.

We can barely bring ourselves to print the shocking truth. But someone has to name and shame.

In a press release issued yesterday, Owen claimed that the New Lanark community was an opportunity 'to commence the most important experiment for the happiness of the human race that had yet been instituted at any time and on any part of the world'. Our report shows that Owen:

OFFERS free health care to his workers
RAISED the minimum age for mill workers from six to a ludicrous twelve
PROVIDES the world's first nursery school
SELLS his workers good food

We say - enough loony lefty nonsense!

Keep cracking the whip over the workers. Or they'll all be after the same thing.

Easier jobs. Better conditions. Education. Lunch breaks. Where will it all end?

Bring back the good old days of dark satanic mills and let's nip this nonsense in the bud once and for all!

Robert Owen is Welsh.

TEN THINGS YOU NEVER KNEW ABOUT KILTS

1. The original form of the kilt owed more to a sari than the modern kilt. It was a very basic garment worn over a shirt, just a strip of plaid cloth which required no tailoring, and known variously as the Breacan, the Feileadh Bhreacain and the Feileadh Mor.

2. *Getting into the original kilt was a bit of a faff. The wearer put his belt on the ground, then put the material over it. Then he plaited the material over the belt until he had gathered along its length, leaving enough at each end to cover the front of his body and overlap each other. Then he lay down on the belt, folded the ends of the kilt over and fastened the belt. The upper part was then fastened on the left shoulder with a large brooch or pin.*

3. The original 'belted plaid' kilt was a multi-purpose garment: it could be used as a cloak in bad weather, and as an overnight blanket if sleeping rough and the tightly woven wool used at the time was almost completely waterproof. In addition it could be easily discarded to allow freedom of movement in a combat situation.

4. *The modern kilt - the 'Feileadh Beg' or little kilt - seems not to have existed before 1725. It is a tailored version of the lower part of the old 'belted plaid'.*

5. Kilt tartan was not originally used for identification of allies; the clan badges worn prominently in the bonnet or balmoral served that function.

6. *At one time the majority of 'Scots' despised the kilt; the Lowlanders regarded it as the garment of primitive barbarians (the Highlanders) who they dubbed 'redshanks', a reference to their legs being cold.*

7. The British government banned the kilt in the aftermath of the 1745 Rebellion, believing it to be an incitement to nationalist pride and further subversion. Offenders were killed or sent to the Colonies. Only those in Highland regiments of the British Armed Services were allowed to wear the kilt and then with strict restrictions.

8. *The balmoral cap is the one most often worn with the kilt, and the headgear most similar to that of the original Highlanders. The diced (or orange checkered) band around the base of the balmoral indicates loyalty to the House of Hanover, that is, the English monarch. Many Scots, particularly Highlanders, do not wear the diced Balmoral, but favour a plain dark blue version.*

9. The Germans rated the kilt-wearing 51st Highland Division as their most formidable opponents in the First World War.

10. *Horrors! The modern 'little kilt' was probably devised by an Englishman, a Mr Rawlinson, manager of an iron smelting works in Lochaber who adapted it to allow more freedom of movement for his workers.*

Key Fact

1817: Publication of *The Scotsman* at 10d a copy - a day's wage for a working man.

Hulloo! Magazine Interviews Glamorous Siege Cannon

MONS MEG

As She Returns Home For Good

CELEBRITY EXCLUSIVE

HULLOO!: A lady never divulges her age, but Mons Meg will make an exception. I can reveal that she dates back to 1457. This formidable siege cannon was presented to King James II by his uncle, Philip the Good, Duke of Burgundy.

HULLOO!: So, Mons Meg, where did you get your name?

MM: I was made at Mons in Belgium, and Meg is short for Margaret. Originally I was one of two siege guns. We were an irresistible pair - in more ways than one.

HULLOO!: Your celebrity grew and in 1497 you had your portrait painted, is that right?

MM: I did indeed. I'm a symbol of Scots military might, and I've got really shapely wheels. The king's flagship Great Michael was painted at the same time. There were rumours of romance between us, but that was all PR fluff.

HULLOO!: When have you been happiest?

MM: Perhaps when I was fired in 1558 to celebrate the marriage of Mary Queen of Scots to the French Dauphin.

HULLOO!: And again you were fired in 1681 to celebrate the birthday of the Duke of Albany - who later became King James VII - weren't you?

MM: Don't remind me! My barrel burst and I had to be repaired. I was black affronted. But there was a time when no ceremonial occasion at Edinburgh Castle was complete without me being brought out with full pageantry, minstrels singing, the lot.

HULLOO!: But it's not all been glamour and smiling for the tourists is it?

MM: Indeed not. I was used against Crookston Castle when the Earl of Lennox rebelled against James IV. And I saw action against the English at the siege of Norham Castle in 1497.

HULLOO!: What was your least favourite job?

MM: Being dragged across the Lammermuirs by James IV to fire across the English border. What a big fat waste of time that was. Just a publicity stunt - 'My siege cannon's bigger than your siege cannon', that kind of thing.

HULLOO!: Why did you retire from active service?

MM: Well I could only be moved at the rate of three miles a day. There were very unkind cracks made about my weight on occasion, I can tell you. But I think six tons is more than reasonable for a curvaceous siege cannon at the height of her charms! Not like these little stick insect cannons they seem to like nowadays. I'm not fat - I'm just big-barrelled.

HULLOO!: What has been your proudest achievement?

MM: I could fire missiles weighing more than 300 lbs over a distance of two and a half miles. That was pretty impressive.

HULLOO!: And now you're coming back to Scotland after a stay in England. How did you get on down south?

MM: I wanted to see if I could make it in the big city so I stayed at the Tower of London for a while, but Edinburgh is where my heart is. It's not a bad place to spend your retirement. I just hope I don't get mobbed by tourists now I'm back.

——— OBITUARY ———
Sir Walter Scott

BORN IN EDINBURGH in 1771, Sir Walter Scott is best known as the man who almost single-handedly invented the modern novel with his sequence, the Waverley Novels. The books were originally published anonymously; Scott was a director of the firm which printed the novels and passed his manuscript to a transcriber. The transcriber could not read Scott's writing and the printers could not read the transcriber's, so the novels never appeared in their intended form in Scott's lifetime.

Scott also vigorously promoted Scottish heritage, inventing the tradition of colour-coded clan tartans as a branding exercise, hiring illiterate peasants to masquerade as clan chiefs and inviting King George IV to visit Scotland in 1822 after Scott's rediscovery of the Scottish regalia.

Scott is therefore responsible for the oceans of tartan tat and singing shortbread tins that substitute for Scottish culture today, including:
* Scary piper dolls in plastic tubes
* Mail order suits of armour
* Woollen Mill shops
* Inedible Edinburgh rock

Thanks, Sir Walter.

It's a Knockout

Anaesthesia Developed by James Simpson

JIMMY SIMPSON from Bathgate has come up with a great invention for all you expectant mums. Anaesthesia! One whiff and you'll be in Seventh Heaven. Now your children will be a pain only when they're growing up - not while you're giving birth!

Ask for it now at your local maternity ward!!!

Jimmy came along to our office to explain how it works

'Now about this anaesthesia. It sounds too good to be true.'

'Aye it does, but it's a simple trick of blocking the channels that take pain from where it hurts to your brain. Although the pain is still there, you don't recognise it.'

The Brimstone Gazette

The Hellfires Are Waiting for You, Mr Simpson

It's an Affront to God-fearing folk. We are born in Pain, we live in Pain and we die in Pain.

James Simpson is the spawn of the De'il for trying to change the world that God Himself made.

> **Key Fact**
>
> At this time, 23 pints of spirit were consumed per head per annum in Scotland. In England it was just seven.

> **Key Fact**
>
> Queen Victoria and Prince Albert built a holiday home at Balmoral in 1855.

It's Greyfriars 'Body'!

THE SQUEAKY-CLEAN image of Greyfriars Bobby was blown away this week with allegations that the children's favourite eats human corpses.

Edinburgh-based Bobby, 14, has been a familiar face in the capital since the death of his owner in 1858. Since that time the faithful terrier has never strayed far from his master's grave.

But now damning rumours have circulated that the dog has

- **FALLEN** in with a disreputable dog gang that hangs around Greyfriars kirkyard
- **SUPPLEMENTED** his diet with human remains interred in the cemetery,

and even

- **DINED** on his master's dead flesh.

Greyfriars Bobby was yesterday unavailable for comment.

OBITUARY

Greyfriars Bobby

GREYFRIARS BOBBY was a small dog allegedly so devastated by the death in 1858 of his master, Midlothian farmer John Gray, that he stood guard over the grave in Greyfriars Kirkyard for the rest of his life. Bobby was fed by staff at nearby Traill's restaurant until his own death in 1872.

Maudlin, misty-eyed sentimentalists who find human relationships too complicated to deal with, and consequently prefer animals to people, have idolised this little dog for years. They totally miss the point that Bobby was in fact a prime example of the Scottish tradition of work-shy defeatist shirkers.

This small but cunning Scot (formerly a working dog, after all) quickly realised that, to secure free board and lodging for the rest of his life and world-wide fame after it, all he had to do was hang around looking dour but loyal (see also: Edinburgh Tourist Guides).

Shipbuilding

Want to earn ££££? Enjoy the fresh air? Come and build ships on the Clyde.

WHETHER YOU HAVE a hankering to build a Puffer or the Queen Mary, we have just the job for you. The Clyde is where it's at. Old-fashioned iron boats are out, stylish steel is in!! Merchant navies and passenger liners across the world, they all love Clyde-built ships.

Work with us you won't regret it; you'll have a great time. No need to go to the gym, we'll give you a workout every day. Then there's the camaraderie, the friendly joking with the sadistic foreman; drink to excess on a Saturday night and when you get home there'll be porridge oats for tea!

But don't hang around much after the beginning of the century, as we'll be going into a decline then.

Key Fact

The Clyde was once full of goldfish. The effluent from the Singer sewing machine factory raised the water temperature sufficiently to allow goldfish - unwanted pets which had been flushed down toilets - to thrive. When the factory closed down, the water temperature fell and the goldfish were unable to survive.

Scots Invented Gothic Fiction

GOTHIC FICTION IS SCOTTISH IN ORIGIN. That's the claim of controversial academic Dr Ceilidh Minogue, who announced her theory while accosting our reporter in Teviot Student's Union yesterday.

'It's all to do with the duality of Scottish character and the dark side of Scottish life,' said Dr Minogue excitedly.

'You just have to look at the classic works of Gothic fiction. They all have Scottish roots. *The Strange Case of Dr Jekyll and Mr Hyde* - the classic treatise on the duality of human nature - written by a Scot, Robert Louis Stevenson, and based on the infamous Deacon Brodie from Edinburgh. Bram Stoker set *Dracula* in Transylvania and Whitby, but he was inspired to write it by a visit to Slains Castle in Grampian. And Mary Shelley spent holidays in Dundee. Look at the opening line of *Frankenstein*: 'It was on a dreary night of November...' - well as anyone who's ever been there will tell you, if that doesn't conjure up a vision of Dundee, I don't know what does.'

Despite our reporter's struggles to escape, she went on 'There are more obviously Scottish examples of Scottish Gothic. Is it any wonder that *The Private Memoirs and Confessions of a Justified Sinner* is James Hogg's best-known work? Or that Robert Burns' masterpiece is his poem *Tam O'Shanter*, which features the Devil himself? Even *The Hound of the Baskervilles*, which uses classic Gothic elements, was written by a Scot, Sir Arthur Conan Doyle.'

'Much modern Scottish writing too reflects this preoccupation with Gothic themes - of the dark undersides to Scottish life. Recent works written or set in Scotland such as *Trainspotting*, *The Wasp Factory* and *Under the Skin* can easily be classed as Gothic.'

Dr Minogue's book on the subject, *Caledonian Gothic*, is in a carrier bag at the end of her bed, along with 47 publishers' rejection slips.

A Clear Guide to Christianity in Scotland

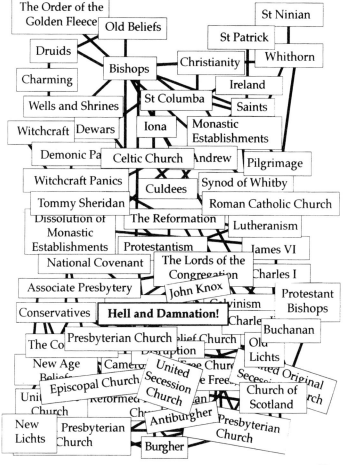

The Order of the Golden Fleece

Old Beliefs

St Ninian

St Patrick

Druids

Christianity

Whithorn

Bishops

Charming

Ireland

Wells and Shrines

St Columba

Saints

Witchcraft Dewars

Iona

Monastic Establishments

Demonic Pa

Celtic Church

Andrew

Pilgrimage

Witchcraft Panics

Culdees

Synod of Whitby

Tommy Sheridan

Roman Catholic Church

Dissolution of Monastic Establishments

The Reformation

Lutheranism

Protestantism

James VI

National Covenant

The Lords of the Congregation

Charles I

Associate Presbytery

John Knox

Protestant Bishops

Conservatives

Hell and Damnation!

Calvinism

Charle

Buchanan

The Co

Presbyterian Church

lief Church

Old Lichts

New Age Beliefs

Camero

United Secession Church

Free Chur

Secess

Original

Episcopal Church

e Free

Church of Scotland

rch

Unit Church

Reformed

an

Presbyterian Church

New Lichts

Presbyterian Church

Antiburgher

Burgher

It's All Downhill from Here

.The Scottish Football Association was founded today in Glasgow

WE TALKED TO some dour and melancholy Scottish Football supporters. 'We don't think much will come of it but grief and disappointment,' said one. 'One hundred years from now, I can see us going off to some far off place like South America for a Football Championship and being humiliated.'

'And don't you know, Angus, it'll cost us an arm and a leg to get there, the tickets will be over priced and the team won't even get into the second round.'

'Personally this Football Association idea is a bad move. Before you know it, we'll have to stand in the cold, eat meat pies every Saturday and then we'll have to go to the pub all evening, locked up in bitter despair.'

'Don't you hate the thought of having to learn chants?'

'Aye, I'm not looking forward to that either.'

'I'm pinning my hopes on the wife forcing me to go shopping or taking the kids to the park.'

'But just think of the pleasure of England winning the World Cup and then the Scotland team thrashing them!'

The thought brings a rare smile to their care-worn faces.

'But it'll never happen!'

'No, you're right there. Well I'd best be off to the bicycle emporium, I'm thinking of buying a rubber inner tube.'

We Say ...

It'll never catch on. No one will want to play it or watch it. Who'd give up their Saturday to go and watch football? Soon there will be a Panopticon Music Hall in Argyll Street: by the 1930s we'll be able to laugh along with Harry Gordon 'the Laird of Invernsecky', there'll be artistes juggling crockery, seals playing musical instruments, Egyptians dancing on sand, amazing memory men, fat musicians with xylophones. We are counting on nude tableaux, but we may need to go Paris for that. There'll be such of a variety of entertainment that no-one will go outside to watch 22 men chase an inflated bladder.

Poet Blamed for Tay Bridge Disaster

IN A BIZARRE TWIST, the designer of the Tay Bridge has blamed a local poet for its collapse. Readers will know of the tragic loss of life: at least 50 passengers were killed when the bridge failed in a storm and they were plunged into the deep waters of the Tay. It had been believed that poor design and substandard work and materials had been the cause of the disaster. Now it emerges that local poet William MacGonagall is being blamed by the bridge's designer, Sir Thomas Bough.

Bough told us: 'There was nothing fundamentally wrong with my design. Perhaps it was a little ambitious, and there was some skimping on materials, but it was strong. We now know that this MacGonagall fellow had composed a poem. The passengers, on seeing the Tay, all got to their feet and recited the line of the poem 'The Tay, the Tay, the silvery Tay'. This outburst caused harmonious motion in the bridge at its natural frequency, which then literally shook itself to pieces. I am vindicated. MacGonagall is to blame.'

William MacGonagall has scoffed at the claim, and retorted:

'About the sad disaster of the Tay,
There really is not very much that one as a poet can say,
To blame my poem is absurd.
This designer Bough fellow is out of his tree and you should give him the bird.'

The Sunday Scone

THE GUID AULD DAYS

What's this craze for running about the streets? Children should be seen and not heard.

Time was, laddies would spend all day at their lessons, then read quietly in the evening.

Now it's all street games, fancy spinning tops and tearing about on carties they make out of scrap wood. The streets are hardly safe any more. If they're not doing that they're chapping on doors and running away.

And if that's not bad enough, they're thieves as well. Stealing apples from folk's gardens and cheeking the bobbies.

Aye. Changed days right enough.

The Smallest Free Church?

More Presbyterians Break Away from the Kirk

INVERNESS-SHIRE CORPORATION has announced that it has found the smallest splinter group of the grim-faced, God-fearing folk. The Independent Church of the Wee Wee Frees has been declared the tiniest sect of all. Founder Willie Arbuthnot is the only member and beats the previous record holder, Ishmael Sutherland of the Little Free Church of Portinnisherrich by virtue of having only one leg. We asked Ishmael what he thought of this and he glared at our reporter for two hours and 12 minutes before handing over a slip of paper denouncing white bread.

Key Fact

The free Presbyterians broke away because they wanted to keep to the strictures of the 1830s and were against the modernising element of the Free Church. The laxity of the Kirk compared to the rigour displayed by many Scots meant that a number of smaller churches were set up. They held extremely strict views about everything. The Bible was taken as the ultimate truth and as such had to be followed to the letter. They took against music and dancing and were fanatical about Sundays.

Letters to the Editor

23rd January 1890

Sir

I have heard rumours that they're going to build a damn great bridge across the Forth. I would like to protest in the strongest terms. What do we need a rail bridge for? It is only going to encourage commercial travellers and the English. We need to stop it now before Scotland is spoilt.

It's time we stood up against the imposition of these monstrous great structures on our doorsteps.

Yes it may cut the journey time to Aberdeen should anyone ever want to go there, yes it may become an attraction for tourists bringing full wallets. But just think of all that steel that will be wasted as the designers over-engineer the thing.

Yours in anger

Tom Brunt Esq

<u>The</u> Sunday Scone

THE GUID AULD DAYS

Time was, laddies made their own fun. We had hours of
enjoyment with a dandelion stalk. Slit the end and hey presto
- a braw wee tooter. You could get a rare wee tune out of it,
imitate birds, play tricks on auld wifies.

And there was more good humour then. Harmless wee
jokes like chicky-melly - chapping on doors and running
away. Or taking a few apples from folk's gardens for a dare.
The bobbies never minded, they kent it was just laddie-like.

And when we'd done that, we made carties out of auld
wood or played with spinning tops. That was all we needed.
We were never bored.

And I mind fine, a tanner ba' would do us. Now they all
want high-falutin' real footballs. Nothing but the best will do,
it seems. They're never happy.

Aye. Changed days right enough.

Famous Scottish Songs
As sung by most Scots

Scotland the Brave

> **Key Fact**
>
> 1901: Launch of Irn Bru - fruit extract
> and iron salt. Renowned as a soft
> drink, mixer for whisky and other
> spirits, and as a hangover cure.

De de de-de de de
De de de de de de
De de de de de de
De de de de de de
De de de de de de
De de de de de de de de

   De de de de de de
   De de de de de de
   De de de de de de de de de
   Land of de de de de de
   Land of de de de de
   Land of de de de de de
   Scotland the brave!

De de de-de de de
De de de de de de
De de de de de de
De de de de de de
De de de de de de
De de de de de de de de

   De de de de de de
   De de de de de de
   De de de de de de de de de
   Land of de de de de de
   Land of de de de de
   Land of de de de de de
   Scotland the brave!

IT'LL NEVER CATCH ON

Scots are well-known as inventors but some of their ideas must have seemed slightly far-fetched, particularly in their home country. Here's a Scottish view of some inventions as they might have been seen at the time...

- A new invention was unveiled today by **Alexander Graham Bell** - the 'telephone'. This is a machine where the voice can be sent down a wire and heard in another room or even another building. What's wrong with opening the window and shouting? When you can send a letter or pay a street urchin to take a message, who needs a daft invention like this?

- **Sir Alexander Fleming** today announced his new discovery - penicillin. This is a 'miracle drug' derived from mould which is claimed to have antibiotic properties. Fleming claims that it has a wide range of applications and will revolutionise the treatment of disease. Nonsense! A good hot toddy and plenty of fresh air is all you need. Imagine trying to cure someone with bits of mould!

- **Sir James Young Simpson** has announced that he is using ether in his obstetric practice to reduce pain - a concept he calls 'anaesthetics'. What's wrong with doing it the usual way? A good shot of whisky and a bash on the head? Anaesthetics indeed.

- **Kirkpatrick Macmillan** today demonstrated his new invention - the 'bicycle'. This is a form of wheeled conveyance which the operator works with pedals to propel it along. Macmillan claims it will enable people to travel swiftly and easily and revolutionise the way they see the world. What a useless gadget. It looks highly uncomfortable, dangerous and tiring to use. What's wrong with walking or taking a horse?

- **John Logie Baird** today demonstrated his apparatus for transmitting a television picture. Baird's 30-line, vertically scanned red and black picture marks the first time a moving image has been transmitted in this way. The inventor claims it will revolutionise the communications and entertainment industry. Television indeed! What's wrong with reading a book, visiting the theatre or going to the pictures?

- **Alexander Wood** the physician today introduced the hypodermic syringe. This is a means of injecting medicine into people via a hollow needle. What's wrong with giving people medicine in spoons? Are peoples' mouths going to disappear or something?

- Scottish mathematician **John Napier** announced today that he has invented the decimal point. This will enable people to write down fractions smaller than one. Decimals indeed! We've managed fine without them til now. So why invent something we didn't need? There's no point to the decimal point.

- **Henry Faulds** has announced his discovery of using fingerprints in forensic work. He claims that, since fingerprints are unique, you can use them to piece together peoples' movements and identify criminals. Fingerprints indeed! How does he know fingerprints are unique? Has he fingerprinted everybody in the world?

- **Joseph Lister**, the eminent surgeon, today announced that his use of antiseptics had dramatically reduced the number of post-operative deaths. His claim is that antiseptic prevents infection. Why not let nature take its course? Or if you're worried about infection, what's wrong with putting a bit of whisky on the wound? Antiseptic indeed.

- **Sir Robert Watson-Watt** has invented radar. Why not just use a telescope?

- **Sir James Dewar** has invented the vacuum flask. He claims it will keep cold drinks cold and hot drinks hot. How can this daft invention possibly do both?

- **William Symington** has developed the first steam-powered marine engine. He claims it can be used to power the world's first paddle steamer. Paddle steamer indeed! Haven't these people heard of oars? Or sails?

- **John Paul Jones** has invented the US navy. What does America need a navy for? Everyone knows Britannia rules the waves.

- **James Chalmers** has invented the adhesive postage stamp. What's the point of that?

- **George Gleghorn** has announced his discovery that quinine bark acts as a cure for malaria. Well that'll come in handy, seeing as how malaria is so rife in Scotland. Why couldn't he have discovered something a bit more useful?

- **Sir William Ramsay** has announced the discovery of the rare gases Helium, Argon, Neon, Krypton and Xenon. He might be better occupied trying to discover a use for them. We've got more than enough gases without people discovering more.

- **Sir Hugh Dalrymple** has announced the invention of hollow-pipe drainage. He claims this innovation will allow the drying of water-logged land, bringing large areas into agricultural production. That'll never work. As soon as the land is dry it will rain and the land will be wet again. That's how it got wet in the first place. Some land is just not meant to be farmed in this way.

- **Alexander Bain** has invented the 'Facsimile'. This is a way of transmitting a copy of something down a telephone wire. What would you need that for?

- **John Loudoun MacAdam** has developed a revolutionary road surfacing process, speeding up transport. Why is everybody in such a rush these days?

- **Charles Mackintosh** has invented a method of waterproofing fabric, so popular that it bears his name. Why do we need that? If it's raining, don't go out.

- **James Watt** is a pioneer in advances in steam engines and a key figure in the industrial revolution. Do we really need all that pollution and all those factories?

Traprain Law Exposé

ENOUGH OF ALL THIS NONSENSE
about the so-called 'fort' at Traprain Law.

The experts tell us it is one of the foremost archaeological
sites in Scotland. They say that excavations have recovered
artefacts from the Neolithic to the Early Historic periods. And
that they have found Roman silver there, now in the Museum
of Scotland.

**Okay, maybe our ancestors did live there. And
perhaps there was a Roman fort.**

But a big boring hill is a big boring hill.

And in a free society it is our God-given right to say so.

MY KIND OF DAY by Johnnie Stark, age 15

*I wake up in our two-room house in the Gorbals, which I share with eleven of
a family including my grandmother, who sleeps on a cot in the corner, and my
parents who sleep in the cavity bed with the baby, who has bronchitis. I pay a
visit to the water closet on the stairway which we share with two other flats
on this landing. It's overflowing again and the Factor won't do anything
about it as we are behind with our rent. Then it's off to work as a coalboy -
my first job. Heaving coal and arguing with old women about money all day
is back-breaking work but it gets me out of the house. After work, I buy a
two-penny packet of cigarettes and meet my mates. We stop to look at the
clabber jigging (pavement dancing) to mouth organ. Later in the day my
father, who's on the dole, goes to the betting shop and loses on the horses. So
he spends the rent money on drink and goes to a 'kipshop' to have a lass for
three shillings. When he comes home he's in a rage as she picked his pocket so
he bashes me on the head with a beer bottle and puts my mother in hospital.
When I wake up, it's time to head off with my mates to Glasgow Green to see
a fight between the Gorbals Razor King and a challenger from Townhead
district. A crowd of close to a thousand spectators and supporters has
gathered. The fight is vicious but broken up by police. When I get home,
father's pawned the clock for more drink and has been arrested in a shebeen,
or illicit drinking house.
There's never a dull moment in the Empire's second city!*

Evil Genius Creates Ultimate Weapon

MAD SCIENTIST JOHN LOGIE BAIRD has almost completed what he calls his 'tele-vision'. 'I will subvert the very fabric of society and hold the world to ransom,' he claimed in a very fuzzy broadcast from his secret hideaway in Glasgow:

'If you don't pay me a thousand guineas and give me my own island somewhere away from the midges and the rain, I will unleash my invention on mankind!'

He added, 'You'll all be sorry then! Your children will be corrupted by creatures such as Muffin the Mule and the Flowerpot Men. Their children will be enslaved by scantily clad women dancing lasciviously to popular music, and by the end of the 20th century your grandchildren will be addicted to badly drawn cartoon figures made cheaply by sweat-shop workers in Japan."

The Prime Minister's office replied that they doubted very much that Mr Baird's vision of the future was likely to occur and dismissed him as a raving madman.

BIRTHS: 25th August 1930

Sean Connery

THE FUTURE FILM STAR **SEAN CONNERY** was born yesterday in Edinburgh, his family announced. Sean - real name Thomas Connery - will shoot to world fame as James Bond in the film *Dr No* in 1962. Sean will make six Bond films in all, although there will be a twelve-year gap between *Diamonds are Forever* and *Never Say Never Again*.

In his career, he will play roles including Alexander the Great, Agamemnon, Richard the Lionheart, Robin Hood, Macbeth and a 2437-year-old Spaniard in *Highlander*. In addition, he will receive an Oscar for *The Untouchables* and become one of the world's busiest film actors. In later life, he will acquire an iconic quality, despite a period in the professional doldrums in the 1980s.

However, success will not come at once for Tollcross's most famous son. His fame will follow years of hard slog as a milkman, a coffin-polisher, a model at Edinburgh College of Art, a lifeguard, a weight lifter, and a chorus boy in musicals.

The infant Sean said today: 'I am looking forward to world fame and will certainly enjoy playing James Bond. It's the sort of part that doesn't come along often and it is going to make my name. Although I get tired of Bond in the end, I don't regret any of my career choices. I'm not looking forward to *Zardoz* much, though.'

Letter of the Week

23rd July 1947

The Proposed Edinburgh Festival

Sir

I must protest about this new-fangled Edinburgh Festival idea. Of all the cack-handed decisions of our worthy city fathers, this must be the most ridiculous. Have the councillors given no thought to how this thing will develop. There doesn't seem to be any harm in a few floppy-wristed young men dancing in private theatres and I have no objection to a good military brass band playing some rousing medleys.

But where will it end? It won't be long before they're setting off fireworks on the castle, there will be jazz played in the streets and that tuneless music of the jungle will soon be frightening our dogs and wives, and turning the milk sour.

Before we know it, there'll be parallel festivals full of long-haired beatniks and young women taking their clothes off. The town will be overrun with tourists demanding fast food and comfortable beds. Stamp it out now before it ruins our fair city.

Your disappointed servant
Tommy Brunt

Key Fact

In the Ian Fleming books, James Bond is half-Scottish, his father being a Scot and his mother Swiss. Bond attended the exclusive Fettes College in Edinburgh after being expelled from Eton.

<u>The</u> Sunday Scone

THE GUID AULD DAYS

Latest thing is, the cinemas are setting up clubs for the youngsters now. The ABC Minors, they cry it. It's even got its own song - All Pals Together or some such.

What's happened to the guid old street games of yesteryear? When I was a lad, we played rare street games. Out in the sun all day long, or playing a game of fitba. Everyone knew each other. You could leave your door open all the time. And go away for a week's holiday leaving it unlocked. Safe as houses.

Now it's all sitting in the cinema watching these fancy talkies. Some of them are even in colour, I hear. And the big thing now is Dan Dare comics and Superman films.

Aye. Changed days right enough.

<u>The</u> Sunday Scone

THE GUID AULD DAYS

What's happened to good old-fashioned heroes? I mind when I was a youngster, Superman was the lad for us. He was someone you could look up to. Someone with true grit.

You would go to the cinema on a Saturday morning and just get in with a jam-jar. See everyone from your school there. Even had our own song. 'We are the ABC Minors, we come along on Saturday mornings ... all pals together...' or something like that. Great days.

Now the laddies are all into this Evel Knievel and skateboards. And if it's not that it's these pop groups.

Aye. Changed days right enough.

Don't Cry For Us in Argentina

THOSE OF US who went off with Ally's army with a smile on their faces and a song in their hearts soon discovered that the Scottish Football team weren't going to let us down. Our lads played appallingly against the lower ranked teams losing 3-1 to Peru and then a typically dismal performance, managing a draw with those giants of world football, Iran. The sight of the opposition scoring both of the goals raised our spirits. To top off a successful start Willie Johnson was then banned for taking a banned substance.

But disappointingly, Scotland rallied, beating Holland the eventual finalists in the competition 3-2. That result together with the judgement that the goal by Archie Gemmell was the best in the competition almost ruined the World Cup for many of us.

It was a disappointing end, but the fans back home were still cheered by this typical display, much relieved that expectations could remain low and that rare successes would seem far more impressive when seen against this background of solid failure.

Lost and Found

We had a number of letters this week claiming the oil found in the North Sea. Thank you for your interest, but it's already been claimed by a Mr Wilson of England.

Festival Knights

Reviews by Sir Ewan Crayford

Macbeth by Gild the Lily Productions

To this radical new version of 'the Scottish Play' with my old mate Sir Scott Hoggswell. Over a Drambuie in the bar, we agreed that this production could not compare with that of 1951. So didn't bother going.

Macbeth Review: *

Drambuie Review: *****

The Mikado by Scot Free Productions

Went along to the new version of *The Mikado*. In the bar, met my old friend Sir Scott Hoggswell. We had a few Glenlivets and discussed the festival. Agreed the quality of this year's shows is terrible. Eventually left the bar when they closed it. Oh yes, we missed the show. Doesn't matter as everyone agrees this year's shows are terrible.

The Mikado Review: *

Glenlivet Review: *****

Rape! Pillage! and Scones for Tea by Whiteworm Productions

More appalling violent rubbish from some idiot under-graduates. What has happened to the clean heroism of the classics? As I said to my good friend Sir Scott Hoggswell, when the Festival started we had *Medea*, *The Duchess of Malfi*, *Hamlet* - none of this blood and gore. Gave it a miss. Jolly good Cardhu malt in the bar though.

Rape! Pillage! and Scones for Tea Review: 0

Cardhu Review: *****

Hamlet by the Really Enthusiastic Spotlights Society of Stirling

Sir Scott Hoggswell and I went along to see this version of Hamlet. Turns out they stage the play in the bar so we had to sit through the wretched thing! Sir Scott and I lined them up before they shut the bar though to make sure we were well oiled before sitting through this piece of amateurism. It was all very confusingly staged and the silly young goats seemed to have missed off the end of the thing! It just seemed to stop at the beginning of the final act! When they opened the bar again everyone was full of complaints about 'the two old toots snoring at the back'. I must have missed that.

Hamlet Review: *

27 Knockando Review: *****

Madame Butterfly by The National Orchestra of Chicago

Magnificent production. The eternal loyalty of Butterfly, abandoned by Pinkerton - the unwanted child - the immortal human pathos - I cannot go on.

Do not miss this show.

Madame Butterfly Review: *****

After-show champagne: *****

Gossamer Kiss by Local Community Theatre

Tawdry rubbish - cliched themes - a stupid girl gets pregnant by a thoughtless soldier - becomes a 'lone mother' sentimentalising the crude lout who has fathered her child - arrant nonsense!

Gossamer Kiss Review: 0

Complimentary Can of Lager Review: *

Letters to the Editor

Scottish Parliament

Sir

I understand that the decision has been taken to reopen the Scottish Parliament. Scotland needs many things but a bunch of freeloaders sitting around jabbering all day and drinking all night is not one of them. We did fine without one for 300 years and think of the money we would save.

It will only encourage weak-minded people to expect a successful football team.

Tom Brunt

tom.brunt@bigot.co.scotland

Postcards from the Old Country
by Diana J. Weinstein III

Visited Bonnybridge, the UFO black spot of Scotland. Apparently there are more UFO sightings here than anywhere else in the world. I'd been watching the skies for hours when I met some friendly young locals. They let me try a local delicacy called 'Buckfast' on condition that I would go into the shop to get them some more. That seemed to bring the UFOs out because I saw strange lights and heard the weirdest noises after that! I had to have some more Buckfast to fortify myself. Then I had an out-of-body experience and woke up by the roadside with a headache and nausea. Could I have been abducted and experimented on by the aliens? Diana

Sun Setting Over the Shale Bings, West Lothian, Scatchland

The Sunday Scone

THE GUID AULD DAYS

Whatever happened to Evel Knievel? He was the boy. Our hero when we were laddies. Where is he now? Thrown aside, that's where. Along with all the braw pop groups of yesteryear.

Now the laddies are all into this World-wide Wrestling Federation and Eminem. And if it's not that it's this Britney Spears.

When I was a lad I would wake up and there was ice on the blankets. Never felt a thing. Didnae care a jot. These youngsters nowadays, they've got it made.

Aye. Changed days right enough.

Postcards from the Old Country
by Diana J. Weinstein III

Hi! Today I am in Edinburgh (that's pronounced Edinburrow, by the way - and the main street is Princess Street). I had to experience the real Scotland so I visited McDonalds, shopped in the Disney Store, and stayed at the Sheraton. Scotland is so welcoming, I felt really at home. Then I went on a bus tour of all the woollen mills - as the tour guide said, when you live in California, you can never have too many sweaters!

Gotta go

Diana

Social Security Office, Fountainbridge, Edinburgh

Still in Edinburgh. Today I visited an exhibition called 'The Edinburgh Experience. I walked in and someone said 'You'll have had your tea.' That seemed to be it.

Diana

Postcards from the Old Country
by Diana J. Weinstein III

Hi guys, today I went to a very swanky restaurant famous for serving MacSween's haggis - the finest you can get in all of Scotland, apparently. I had seen toy haggis in the gift shops but is it a bird or a hedgehog or what? I asked the waiter and he told me this cockamamie story about how they live in the Highlands and have three legs, with one long and two short so they can run round the hills. Well I didn't believe a word of it but guess what, they had a whole one in the kitchens. Sure enough, it has three legs. They look a little like chicken wings, but you could see that one was long and two were short. I wouldn't have believed it if I hadn't have seen it for myself. I guess it pays to have an open mind! More next time

Diana

Multi-storey car park, King Stables Road, Edinburgh

SCOTLAND
——— THE MOVIE ———

Explore ten thousand years of history in a single film.

A castle, actually in Ireland, which looks Scottish

More epic than *Gladiator*.
More gory than *Hannibal*.
More confusing than *Lord of the Rings*.

A Cast of Thousands, including:

Calgacus EWAN McGREGOR Robert the Bruce EWAN McGREGOR William Wallace EWAN McGREGOR
Rob Roy EWAN McGREGOR Mary, Queen of Scots EWAN McGREGOR Robbie Burns EWAN McGREGOR
Macbeth EWAN McGREGOR Saint Columba EWAN McGREGOR Bonnie Prince Charlie EWAN McGREGOR
Flora MacDonald EWAN McGREGOR James I-VII EWAN McGREGOR Jim Baxter EWAN McGREGOR
Loch Ness Monster EWAN McGREGOR Ben Nevis EWAN McGREGOR Sean Connery HIMSELF
Scotland PINEWOOD STUDIOS, England, AND IRELAND
Made without the help of VISIT 'We holiday abroad' SCOTLAND

114

Beer will be Free in 2003

THE SCOTCH INDEPENDENCE PARTY (SIP) has pledged that should they win independence in 2003 they will make beer free. This will include all lagers, cask-conditioned ales and stout and even Guinness. 'We are in no way wanting to put Scottish products first,' said Hamish MacSporran, spokesperson for the party. 'Guinness, German lager, as well as Belgian, Spanish and Dutch, and American non-EU drinks will all be free as well as our traditional 70 and 80 shilling and lagers, export, special and guest beers.'

This comes on the tail of promising that the sun will shine over the summer months (although it will rain late at night, just to water the grass and plants and stuff you understand: they do not want an English-style drought), and that cancer will be cured and everyone will live to at least 120 years old in health, happiness and great wealth.

Meanwhile, New Once-Socialist-But-No-More-Never-No-More Party have revealed how they intend to counter the aggressive new tactics of the SIP. 'Well,' said Alasdair MacKeich, 'we will attack the SIP on their divisive policies and show people the benefits they have from maintaining the union of Scotland and England, such as, er, hearing English cricket and English football scores, supporting the subsidy junkies of the south-east of England, finding out that severe weather only affects the south of England, hearing about laws and news which only affect England, being ignored and derided by the English, putting up with Wee Blue Rinse Englanders, and watching fascinating repeats of the 1966 World Cup Final when England won. 'They think it's all over: it is now.' If only that was true how all Scotland would rejoice!'

The Blue Rinse Party have also reacted to the SIP policy with their manifesto 'Blue Scotland – Screwing a Jelly to the Ceiling'. 'We will not only have free beer,' said their spokesman Plantagenet Sleaze, 'we will give you a tenner and quickie round the back if you vote for us.'

Scotland Wins World Cup

THE SCOTTISH FOOTBALL team confounded everyone by winning the World Cup, in a brilliant display beating England 7-0 in the final.

People throughout Scotland were stunned: shops closed, businesses abandoned, streets filled with dazed people, wandering about aimlessly, some weeping and tearing out their hair.

One passer-by spoke for the nation: 'Sadistic fiends! This is impossible. We have been a nation that revelled in failure and collective gloom. What are we going to do? I just want to scream.'

Meanwhile, the team manager has fled the country, and the team has gone into hiding after receiving death threats from fans.

Visit

Terra Scotia (Scotland)

for the Holiday of a Lifetime

One year after its separation from the British Isles, the floating island Terra Scotia (formerly Scotland) has reached its new home off the coast of Spain and is ready to receive visitors. First Minister Kadiatu McGregor said 'This is the most exciting development ever in the history of Scottish tourism. A Mediterranean climate will really enable Scotland to compete with other resorts. And the new attractions we are opening put Scotland in the very forefront of world tourism.'

Concerns about the coastal erosion that has already led to the loss of Glasgow, Edinburgh and Dundee led some commentators to speculate that the island could not sustain the stress of the journey. However, architects involved with the flotation of the island were reported to be 'delighted and relieved' at its stability. Since its separation from the rest of Britain, the island has made its slow journey to its new mooring site off the coast of southern Spain.

Terra-forming work done over the last twenty years includes:
- The relocation of major landmarks of Glasgow and Edinburgh to the new capital city, Crieff
- The landscaping of the Highlands
- The construction of inland beaches with full tidal control

The Sean Connery Hotel is now open and offers a range of traditional Scottish experiences, including:

- Golf World - featuring Crazy Golf, Underwater Golf and Zero Gravity Golf
- The Smoking Dome - visit facsimile Scottish pubs and experience the authentic twentieth-century atmosphere (oxygen treatment available. Visits limited to ten minutes at a time.)
- Concerts of Scottish classical music, including Gaelic folk music, Highland pipe bands and Travis
- The Cholesterol Restaurant - where you can step back in time and sample controlled substances such as whisky, chips, Scotch pies and sugar
- Historical re-enactments including ritual razor fights on a recreation of Glasgow Green

Take a trip to the Highlands, now landscaped and repopulated with stags, bears and wolves: so remember not to leave your skimmers if you visit this region.

Visit the shrine of Scotus: the Pharaoh's daughter who brought the Stone of Destiny to Scotland and gave the country its name.

See the Loch Ness Monster legend brought to life: Loch Ness is now stocked with a herd of genetically engineered plesiosaurs to take you back to Scotland's earliest days.

And enjoy Scotland's history recreated: the battles of Culloden and Bannockburn are performed twice daily by holographic armies.

___ **YES, I would like to take this opportunity to book my holiday** (please note that this advert refers to holidays not available until 3000 AD). **I enclose a cheque for £100,000** (to account for inflation) as my booking fee along with the genetic code of my descendant who will take the holiday. Please note no refunds are available, and booking fees cannot be returned. Still, if you want to send us some money, please do so. We are a small business operating in a competitive market place and free money would be excellent: thank you in advance.

Send your cheque (made out to '**Goblinshead**') to TERRA SCOTIA HOLIDAYS, c/o Goblinshead 130B Inveresk Road, Musselburgh EH21 7AY, Scotland.

Name _____ Address _____

Town _____ Post Code _____ Planet _____

TERRA SCOTIA (Scotland): Book now for the holiday of a lifetime!

Expand Your Vocabulary
With Scottish Place Names

Aberdour: A concentrated form of dour, only reached by tantric masters in the art. Think Victor Meldrew, Scotty (in the original Star Trek only) and the Sunday Post leader writer.

Alloway: To depart after a night's drinking.

Arbroath: To yearn for, especially smoked fish.

Athelstaneford: Incontinence caused by sneezing.

Auchindrain: Exclamation made when jewellery, spectacles, keys etc accidentally fall down toilet.

Bolfracks: Nasty injury that happens when you jump onto a bike and miss the saddle.

Broughty: Similar to draughty but also smells vaguely of sewage.

Butt of Lewis: A reference to a particularly pert Galloway farmer of the 1790s and now used to describe any cantilevered structure. As immortalised in Robert Burns' poem 'You could balance your pint on the Butt of Lewis'.

Chicken Head: Scrawny and slightly backward child.

Crathes: The feeling you get when you have to walk about all day after visiting a toilet with no loo roll.

Duddo: One-night stand who passes out in the middle of the crucial act.

Duff House: Quite nice actually.

Dunbog: Vast feeling of relief experienced on just making it to the toilet in an airport.

Dundee: To yearn for, especially sweet food.

Farkill: Emotion experienced upon not making it to the toilet in an airport.

Farquhar: To mutter expletives; derived from Farquharson.

Flodigarry: Description of the floor of bus station toilets.

Flotta: Anything which can not be flushed from a toilet bowl.

Forfar: To yearn for, especially pastie-type savouries.

Fyvie: Sinking feeling produced on realising pay day is too far away to cope with your current rate of spending.

Glenduckie: Site of the first gay pub in Scotland, as evidenced by Pictish inscriptions of 'Steps' dance routines and telephone numbers.

Gourock: A cough with very thick phlegm.

Greenknowe: Stage in a cold or flu at which mucous becomes thick and discoloured.

Greenock: A cough with discoloured phlegm.

Hawick: A spasmodic and productive cough.

Hosh: The extremely loose stools produced by a night drinking nothing but red wine.

Inchcolm: To brush the hair very slowly.

Inchkeith: The act of spending a long time on the toilet.

Inchmickerie: A very small practical joke.

Inverquharity: A feeling of well being or good health.

Kilchurn: Uneasy feeling that you may need to make an urgent and inconvenient trip to the toilet when in an airport.

Lorn: To yearn for, especially meat products.

Lurg Hill: Any outdoor geographical feature behind which one can be sick.

Maggieknockater: Pedlar who comes to your door selling things and unpacks everything at lightning speed, so you have to buy something off her in order to see your doorstep again.

Meikle Wartle: An unpleasant condition which can, however, be treated by painting it (or them) with lotion or freezing with liquid nitrogen.

Mellerstain: Marks left on Lady Chatterley's clothing by her gamekeeper.

Menteith: Poor dental hygiene.

Moffat: (1) To make a mess of things (2) To kiss a woman (slang).

Muckhart: To denounce or insult an item.

Nigg: Egg of headlice.

Old Meldrum: To be especially grumpy.

Portnockie: (1) Importer of Italian food (2) Place where sailors go for relief (slang).

Skipness: The lightness of heart you feel when you are in love or have just won some money on the Lottery.

Slacks of Cairnbanno: Similar to 'Essex girls' but less able to hold their drink.

Smoo: Residue under the waterline in a toilet.

Tain: (1) To hang around the chip shop on a weekend night (2) To hang around the chip shop on any night.

Tantallon: Bright orange woman with nail extensions, usually found selling expensive lard-in-a-jar skin care in swanky Edinburgh stores.

Thirlestane: To experience a giddy feeling when standing up too quickly.

Threave: To cut a cake tactically so you get the biggest part.

Threepwood: Wood from Threep, would you believe?

Thurso: To wake up thinking it is Saturday morning, then realise it is actually Friday.

Trotternish: Frequent trips to toilet necessitated by food poisoning.

Urquhart: To mutter expletives under the breath.

Become More Caledonian at

The Braveheart Academy of Scottishness

Patrons: Victor Meldrew and Private Fraser

First, take this short test: HOW SCOTTISH ARE YOU?

Being Scottish is not an accident of birth or a fact of geography - it's a state of mind.
Wherever you live, you might actually be Scottish. Try this quiz to find out!

1. Does a good night out include:
A   A nice meal in a restaurant
B   A play or a new movie
C   A fight

2. When were you most happy?
A   When Scotland beat England at football
B   When Germany beat England at football
C   At a funeral

3. Complete this saying: It's nice weather but...
A   Will it cost me anything?
B   We're all doomed
C   We'll pay for it

4. Is your favourite meal:
A   Haggis, neeps and tatties
B   A slap-up meal in a restaurant
C   Wrapped in newspaper

5. Is your favourite hobby:
A   Hill walking
B   Football
C   Moaning

6. Is your favourite place:
A   The Highlands of Scotland
B   Castles and fine buildings
C   Public bar of 'The Volunteer Arms'

7. What do you drink:
A   The finest malt whisky
B   Wine and beer
C   Rocket fuel

8. How much exercise do you take:
A   Regular exercise twice a week
B   Play football every so often
C   Lifting the remote control

9. Which part of a newspaper do you turn to first:
A   Politics and current affairs
B   Sport or the jobs page
C   Obituaries and weather forecast

10. If you were diagnosed with a life-threatening illness would you:
A   Seek the best treatment
B   Tell everyone about it endlessly
C   Be glad that it will all be over soon

How did you score?

Mostly As: You're not very Scottish at all, are you? Perhaps you should cut down on your anti-depressants.

Mostly Bs: Getting there. Perhaps you live in the Borders or some part of the world with really bad weather. Quite Scottish in outlook - but must try harder!

Mostly Cs: Congratulations! You are so Scottish you could be sold in a plastic tube in any shop on Edinburgh's Royal Mile.

Mostly As and Bs? You need to brush up your Scottishness by attending the Braveheart Academy of Scottishness.

Become More Caledonian at

The Braveheart Academy of Scottishness

**We offer a variety of courses to suit everyone,
from the expatriate with a slightly Scottish name
to the full Scot in need of a refresher course.**

Just Some of the Skills You Will Learn:
* Complaining in restaurants (Basic)
* Complaining in restaurants (Advanced)
* Heavy sighs
* Meaningful pauses
* Distrust of all strangers

Enhance Your Vocabulary with A Host of Scottish Phrases
* Nae guid'll come o' this
* I'm no' long for this world
* God willing, and if I'm able
* If I'm spared

Scottish Inventors Night Class
Astound your friends by claiming Scottish inventors discovered everything under the sun. Other courses just list television, telephone and penicillin. We cover:
* Scotch Eggs
* Scotch Tape
* Scotland Yard
* Scotch Corner
* Dilithium

Courses to Suit All Ages

Under 50? Take our Dour Studies course. Learn how to predict the worst - and be right; how to find the cloud in every silver lining; and how to successfully conceal your emotions from your loved ones for your entire life.

Over 50? Why not choose our Advanced Maudlin course. Sink into depression as you realise you have wasted your life. And crawl into that whisky glass at the end of the course.

Scottish Master Class
For the fully experienced Scot, an opportunity to study advanced Scottishness to degree level. Includes:
* Pointing out flaws
* Cadging drink and fags
* Rubbishing anyone who is successful
* Testing to destruction
* Sectarianism
* Relishing obituaries
* Forecasting (bad) weather

For a full prospectus write to the **Braveheart Academy of Scottishness**, c/o Goblinshead, 130B Inveresk Road, Musselburgh, EH21 7AY.

Please note we will not reply unless as mentioned below*. If you want, however, send us as much money as you can. Please note you will get nothing in return, not even a receipt or a reply (*unless it is to ask you for more money), and certainly not a thank you. We will simply keep your money, and then deride you with how stupid and gullible some people are, especially those who are not *true* Scots. Be assured, though. As *true* Scots we believe that no good can come from you giving us money. So even if we spend it we will not enjoy it. Promise.

Famous Scottish Songs
As sung by most Scots

Auld Lang Syne

Should old acquaintance be forgot,
And never brought to mind,
Should old acquaintance be forgot,
For the sake of old lang syne

For old lang syne, my dear,
For auld lang syne
For old lang syne, my dear,
For auld lang syne

Should old acquaintance be forgot,
And never brought to mind,
Should old acquaintance be forgot,
For the sake of old lang syne

For old lang syne, my dear,
For auld lang syne
For old lang syne, my dear,
For auld lang syne

Should old acquaintance be forgot,
And never brought to mind,
Should old acquaintance be forgot,
For the sake of old lang syne

For old lang syne, my dear,
For auld lang syne
For old lang syne, my dear,
For auld lang syne